A WAR ON TERROR

Afghanistan and After

Paul Rogers

T0190520

Pluto Press

LONDON • STERLING, VIRGINIA

First published 2004 by Pluto Press
345 Archway Road, London N6 5AA
and 22883 Quicksilver Drive, Sterling, VA 20166–2012, USA

www.plutobooks.com

British Library Cataloguing in Publication Data
A catalogue record for this book is available from the British Library

ISBN   0 7453 2087 2 hardback
ISBN   0 7453 2086 4 paperback

Library of Congress Cataloging in Publication Data
Rogers, Paul, 1943–
   A war on terror : Afghanistan and after / Paul Rogers.
      p. cm.
   ISBN 0–7453–2087–2 — ISBN 0–7453–2086–4 (pbk.)
   1. War on Terrorism, 2001– 2. Terrorism—Government policy—United
States. 3. National security—United States. 4. United States—Foreign
relations—2001– I. Title.
   HV6432 .R64 2004
   973.931—dc22

                                                          2003018193

10   9   8   7   6   5   4   3   2   1

Designed and produced for Pluto Press by
Chase Publishing Services, Fortescue, Sidmouth, EX10 9QG, England
Typeset from disk by Stanford DTP Services, Northampton, England
Printed and bound in Canada by Transcontinental Printing

Contents

Acknowledgements

My main thanks go to the people who make *openDemocracy* happen. As one small part of their activities, and on a weekly basis, they turn my contributions into finished articles, embedding a range of links to other sites in the process (www.opendemocracy.com). Special thanks go to Anthony Barnett who got me involved in this endeavour in the first place, but I greatly appreciate the help of all of the staff, especially David Hayes, Susan Richards, Bola Gibson, Caspar Henderson and Rosemary Bechler.

Over the period covered by this book I have been involved with the Oxford Research Group, a remarkable group of people who work with policy formers on nonviolent alternatives to conflict and achieve notable results on a minimal budget. Working with Scilla Elworthy of ORG has resulted in a series of reports on the impact of 9/11 and the subsequent 'war on terror', and the discussions and advice from ORG staff in connection with these has been an invaluable source of ideas for analysing events.

In trying to make some kind of sense of the 'war', it has been extraordinarily helpful to have had so many discussions with staff and students in the peace studies department at Bradford University. Photocopies of relevant articles appear as if by magic, missed news items are pointed out, and disagreements kindly voiced.

I have worked with one of my colleagues, Malcolm Dando, over a number of years. Immediately after the World Trade Center and Pentagon attacks, Malcolm said to me that the real significance of the tragedies would be that it would enable the Pentagon 'hawks' and their associates to do whatever they wanted. Nearly two years later, that remains the case.

Paul Rogers
4 August 2003

Introduction

OpenDemocracy began as an independent not-for-profit web journal early in 2001. It developed over 18 months into a widely read international source of information on ideas before its more formal launch on 4 November 2002. Since then it has grown substantially and has a readership numbering in the many tens of thousands stretching across the world. It describes itself as 'a channel for knowledge, learning, participation and understanding that is not owned by a media corporation, does not serve a special interest and does not adhere to a single ideological position'. It intends to be a vehicle for democratic change and for closing the gap between people and power, and maintains an emphasis on dialogue and the sharing of knowledge 'across borders and differences'.

Following an initial commentary on the immediate consequences of the attacks in New York and Washington on 11 September 2001, one of the columns established on the website was concerned with global security, the intention being to try and attempt an ongoing analysis, on a weekly basis, of the anticipated war in Afghanistan and the wider US responses to the 9/11 attacks.

In an earlier book (*Losing Control*), I argued that unless the United States responded uncharacteristically after 9/11, looking for underlying causes rather than concentrating almost entirely on rigorous counter-terrorism actions, it would lead all of us, including itself, into a world of greater chaos. So it has proved, and since 9/11 the *openDemocracy* columns have sought to chart the development of the 'war on terror', with all of the problems that have arisen.

The Global Security column has become an established feature of *openDemocracy* and has covered a wide range of themes. They include issues such as missile defence, the weaponisation of space, nuclear strategy and the South Asian confrontation, but the primary concern has been with the aftermath of 9/11, the US security posture, Afghanistan, the Middle East and President Bush's 'war on terror'.

Many of the conclusions have proved correct or partially correct and some have proved wrong – you must judge for yourself. Hopefully, and in a world of turmoil, this book will help provide a record for people concerned with world affairs, a record they can identify with and relate to.

The emphasis throughout is on trying to analyse and understand what is happening on all of these issues, more or less as they happen, and to try and predict their implications for the near-term and even for the more distant future. Lacking any advantage of hindsight, this is a risky thing to attempt, but it does have the advantage that the columns, as they accumulate, give a sense of what appeared to be most significant at the time. Often, in later examinations of issues of peace and conflict, events and people that were significant at the time can easily be sidelined. 'Real time analysis', as in these articles, may help to avoid that and assist in maintaining a more comprehensive perspective. As such, they may serve to complement the more conventional forms of analysis produced months, years or decades after the events they seek to understand.

It was in the hope that such an approach might be of use that this collection of articles from the Global Security column of *openDemocracy* is published here. The individual columns are reproduced almost exactly as published, with just minor grammatical corrections and some avoidance of repetition, but no adjustments in analysis. They are grouped into seven chapters, each with an introduction to set them in context.

This set of articles covers the period from October 2001 to December 2002 and concentrates primarily on Afghanistan, Israel-Palestine, the United States and al-Qaida and its associates. Some mention is made of the developing crisis with Iraq, but that is in many ways a separate and very substantive issue. It is not central to this particular set of articles and perhaps deserves more detailed attention on another occasion.

1
War in Afghanistan – I

Almost immediately after the 9/11 attacks on New York and Washington, the al-Qaida network was identified as responsible for the atrocities, and its host Taliban regime in Afghanistan was thus seen as a prime part of the enemy in President Bush's declared 'war on terror'. There was therefore some surprise that the war against the Taliban in Afghanistan did not start for several weeks. People remembered President Clinton's rapid use of cruise missiles against targets in Sudan and Afghanistan in response to the bombing of US embassies in East Africa, and there was an expectation of immediate retaliation.

In practice, such attacks would have been little more than symbolic, and the US military therefore developed plans for much more substantial military action, aware of the requirement to finish the war before the onset of winter. The main problems for the military were the lack of nearby bases from which to launch an attack, and the risk to US troops of engaging in ground conflict against Taliban and al-Qaida guerrilla forces.

This chapter records developments over the first eight weeks of the war and shows the importance of the use of Northern Alliance forces in combination with US air power. Essentially, the United States took the option of taking sides in the long-running Afghanistan civil war, even though the human rights record of the Northern Alliance was little better than that of the Taliban.

For the first four weeks of the war, there appeared to be little progress with the US war aims, but the impact of the rearming of the Northern Alliance forces in combination with the US bombing campaign was crucial and ultimately had its effect. At the same time, and even within just a few weeks of the start of the war, two other issues were becoming apparent. One was that there were significant civilian casualties being caused, partly through targeting errors and partly through the use of area impact munitions (AIMs). The other was that there were already signs that the Taliban and al-Qaida groups were frequently withdrawing rather than fighting, a tactic that was to have long-term significance, given that the US military had little interest in a lengthy presence in Afghanistan.

In the wider 'war on terror', there were already firm indications that the security hawks in Washington had their sights set on the Saddam Hussein regime in Iraq. There were also two further developments that provided markers for the future. One was the substantial number of people taken into custody in the United States, coupled with a presidential directive establishing military courts for the trial of foreign nationals. The other was the decision to allow the CIA to undertake assassinations of presumed terrorists overseas.

From Afghanistan to Iraq?
15 October 2001

Although most of the media has given an impression of a massive air bombardment, the reality is of a fairly low-level air war, for two different reasons. Firstly, the United States is unable to use bases in the region for bombers or strike aircraft, only for special operations forces, reconnaissance aircraft and drones, or special functions such as aerial refuelling. It is therefore reliant on aircraft flying from carriers operating well offshore in the Arabian Sea, from Diego Garcia or, in the case of the B-2 stealth bomber, from bases in the United States. As a result, on some recent nights, fewer than ten targets were attacked.

While the B-2 bombers deliver large numbers of bombs, they fly from the US to Afghanistan and then on to Diego Garcia, where fresh crews fly them back to the US. The whole sortie takes nearly 70 hours, the planes need detailed maintenance and the US only has 21 of them, with perhaps 14 operational at any one time. It is unlikely they can use more than three in any one night.

Strike aircraft launched from carriers need aerial refuelling. The carriers have a limited number of small tanker aircraft, but the US is also relying on RAF tankers flying out of Oman. Extraordinary as it might seem, USAF tankers are not configured to refuel US Navy planes. Such operational difficulties severely limit the capability of the US to maintain aircraft loitering over Afghanistan looking for 'targets of opportunity'.

The second reason for the limited strikes is that there are few readily available targets. The Taliban regime is not configured like a conventional army and air force – there are very few planes and helicopters and few large barracks or troop concentrations. The forces are essentially infantry and guerrilla forces. Their mode of operation stems from the Soviet occupation of the 1980s, when Afghan resistance groups found it effective to organise in dispersed groups of 20–200 fighters.

In the last few days, air defences and mostly obsolete aircraft have been destroyed quickly, and the primitive command and control systems have also been damaged, as have the few bunkers that might have housed military commanders. Most of these are of no great value to the Taliban – in one case, a number of aircraft were destroyed on the ground in an air raid, but they had not been flown for more than a decade.

The limits of technology

Attempts have been made to target troop concentrations, and the US is now using 'area impact munitions' (AIMs) such as cluster bombs for this purpose. As the name implies, these are at the opposite end of the bombing spectrum from precision-guided laser bombs. They are designed from the start to cause destruction over the greatest area, and are used against 'soft' targets such as trucks, tented camps and people. A typical cluster bomb is actually a canister that dispenses around 150 'bomblets', each of which detonates to spread up to 2,000 high-velocity shrapnel fragments, the whole bomb shredding anything or anyone within a couple of acres.

Use of AIMs, especially from high altitude, means that civilian casualties are virtually certain. In any case, up to 10 per cent of cluster bomb munitions can fail to detonate, leaving behind what amount to anti-personnel land mines. Such bomblets have resulted in numerous injuries and deaths months and years after their use in the 1991 Gulf War, and will do so likewise in Afghanistan.

Even without the use of AIMs, there have been problems with targeting precision-guided bombs. Incidents include the deaths of four UN workers early last week and two more recent events, one possibly involving more than 100 people killed. One reason may be that the National Imaging and Mapping Agency (NIMA) falls massively short of producing the digital databases that are needed to guide the bombs. These are rather like finely defined maps; they should give three-dimensional targeting co-ordinates accurate to within nine metres. According to a reliable report, regional commanders need 9,000 of these 'maps' to provide adequate coverage. As of late September, they were 5,000 short of this figure.

In other moves, the US Navy is ordering 600 more sea-launched cruise missiles to replace stocks used in recent years against Iraq, Sudan, Serbia and Afghanistan. It is also asking for $4 billion in emergency spending on base and ship security. There is currently a worry that the massive aircraft carriers in the Arabian Sea might be subject to suicide attacks, analogous to the New York and Washington attacks.

What next?

The bombing may continue for some days, possibly with a pause to see if the Taliban will give up bin Laden (this seems unlikely, though they may make offers chiefly for propaganda purposes). Targets will become more difficult to find. There are indications that many Taliban units have been ordered to disperse into cities, towns and villages to await American ground troops. The al-Qaida network has up to 55 bases throughout Afghanistan, but these are not so much fully-fledged bases as locations used often on a temporary basis.

Meanwhile, there is a divergence in Washington between military chiefs and the Pentagon's politicians. The military want to continue the bombing rather than risk their elite Special Forces in any numbers, in view of the risk of a costly guerrilla war with winter coming on. Their political masters want Special Forces action. Increasingly, they see the military as out of touch with political realities.

Within Afghanistan, there is considerable integration of the bin Laden forces into the Taliban armed forces. There is little doubt that they, too, will have spread out widely. There are also reports that much of the network has dispersed, many of its personnel even quietly leaving Afghanistan for neighbouring countries to the north and east. A dispersal could last months or years. Given local support in countries such as Pakistan, network personnel would be almost impossible to track down. If the US does deploy forces in Afghanistan in pursuit of al-Qaida, there may be little to find.

In the immediate future, the US will attempt to seek and destroy units of the Taliban's 55th Brigade, several thousand troops including many Arabs and other foreign supporters. While this is the most effective Taliban group, it is reported to be widely spread, with only a few hundred concerned with guarding the al-Qaida leadership (including bin Laden). The use of helicopter-borne troops and AC-130 gunships is likely. But there is no certainty that the 55th Brigade and other elements of the Taliban militia can be found and attacked within the next four weeks, before the start of Ramadan and then the onset of winter.

According to the US Secretary of Defense, Donald Rumsfeld, 'continuous pressure' will be maintained on the Taliban and elements of the network, but the limited availability of air bases in the region from which to operate makes this questionable. Moreover, the use of Pakistani bases even for helicopter and Special Forces operations may become problematic, given the current development of opposition to the US military operations in Pakistan.

It is possible that the Taliban might still give up bin Laden. It is also possible that a US air strike or Special Forces operation might destroy him and the network leadership. Both are unlikely. It is more probable that the war will continue for several weeks before being scaled down over the winter. During a much longer timeframe of several months, the extent of troop movements from the United States will give a clear indication of whether the US is planning major and persistent military interventions in Afghanistan next year.

The region, especially Iraq

Street-level opposition to US action is growing in a number of countries in the Middle East and South-west Asia. States such as Pakistan and Jordan are moving fast to detain the more militant local leaders. Such action may ensure short-term stability at the risk of longer-term problems, especially if the war stretches over many months.

On the other hand, intense US pressure on Israel is having some effect – the Israeli army has withdrawn armoured units from key areas around Hebron, and two hard-line members of Sharon's cabinet are likely to resign their posts in protest.

Among the Arab states, Saudi Arabia is particularly sensitive, especially in relation to possible military action against Iraq. A powerful group in Washington sees as essential an Iraq offensive, combining extensive air strikes with, in due course, military occupation of Iraq's southern oilfields, support for Kurdish rebels in the north and Shi'ite forces in the south. While the latter action would be months away, there are reports of the build-up of substantial Turkish armed forces units on the Turkish-Iraqi border. This might be part of such a plan, but could instead be designed to prevent Iraqi Kurds linking up with Kurdish opposition forces in southeast Turkey.

The group of US hawks centres around the Defense Policy Board (DPB), a bipartisan group of hard-line security advisers. These include Richard Perle, Newt Gingrich, Henry Kissinger, Dan Quayle, and former CIA Director James Woolsey, who has recently been in Britain seeking evidence of an Iraqi link with 11 September. Both Donald Rumsfeld and his deputy Paul Wolfowitz attended a recent two-day meeting of the DPB that largely excluded participation from the State Department (which takes a much more cautious view, as does the UK government).

Faultlines

The war is in its early stages, is taking place in a region of hugely complex politics and is following a course that is extraordinarily difficult to predict. Even so, four issues are relevant:

- There are substantial limitations on US military action because of the unavailability of local bases.
- Opposition to the United States in the region is growing quite rapidly.
- The al-Qaida network is being more successful than expected in portraying the war as 'the west versus Islam'.
- A powerful lobby in Washington wants to extend the war to Iraq.

The 'Iraq hawks' will probably not succeed, not least because of opposition from the Saudi authorities who fear strong internal opposition to any such US move. This, though, is the very reason why the Saddam Hussein regime may deliberately seek to provoke such a reaction, either by substantial infringements of the no-fly zones or else by an apparent military move towards Kuwait. While all the attention is being paid to the conflict in Afghanistan, it is worth watching Iraq.

An elusive enemy
22 October 2001

From early in the third week of the war, the United States was able to operate strike aircraft such as the F-15 out of Uzbekistan. This has enabled the US to mount more air raids and has partially overcome the previous limitations of using carrier-based aircraft and long-range bombers. Even so, press reports of up to 100 aircraft involved in air strikes in any one day are misleading, as the number actually dropping bombs is much smaller. Aircraft involved include tankers, electronic countermeasures planes, 'back-up' strike aircraft, interceptors engaged in combat air patrols, and reconnaissance aircraft. These can make up 70 per cent of the total aircraft used.

Even so, the US now has a greater ability for airborne intervention, although Gulf and Pakistani bases still do not appear to be available for bombing. The movement of a fourth aircraft carrier into the region appears to indicate an acceptance of the need to use carrier air-power into the winter.

Widening the targets

Use of area impact munitions such as cluster bombs has been confirmed, and the AC-130 gunship is also designed to have an area impact effect. The use of such munitions against possible Taliban military concentrations is highly likely to lead to much larger civilian casualties. In the past two weeks there have been at least six cases of mis-targeting, including UN and Red Cross facilities.

Kandahar has clearly experienced widespread damage that goes beyond the targeting of military sites. This does fit in with patterns of US air attacks in previous wars such as the Gulf War and Serbia, where the definition of 'military' is capable of being greatly stretched to include targets that serve a primarily civil function (transport nodes, power stations, administration offices, radio stations).

An effect of this is to degrade the capability of a city or other urban area to provide electricity, drinking water and other facilities for its population, making refugee flows more likely. These, in turn, make civilian casualties more likely, especially as Taliban military movements become mixed in with refugees. Even so, US bombing strategy is still not as harsh as the out-and-out destruction carried out by the Russians in Chechnya. At the same time, US forces may yet use fuel-air explosives (sometimes called thermobaric weapons) against underground bunkers and trenches. These were used against Iraqi positions in the Kuwaiti desert and are particularly destructive. The Russians have used them in urban areas in Chechnya.

The Northern Alliance

There are credible reports that the Northern Alliance is starting to receive substantial quantities of arms from Russia, possibly financed by the US. In return for this, and other aid, the United States is unlikely to criticise Russian suppression in Chechnya, and improving US relations with China may give Beijing more of a free rein against Islamic rebels in western regions. Both moves will further inflate antagonism to the United States in a number of Islamic countries.

While the Northern Alliance is being strengthened, there remains unwillingness on the part of Washington to see it move on Kabul, not least because it does not carry support in Afghanistan as a whole. Thus, if the immediate aim is to cause the collapse of the Taliban regime, an acceptable alternative regime is not readily available.

The media

There is a dearth of reliable information coming out of Afghanistan, and direct media access to US forces is under remarkably strict control. As a consequence, media manipulation is easy and a noteworthy feature of the first two weeks has been a careful 'feeding' of stories, day by day, with an emphasis on items that produce good graphics. The AC-130 gunship was one example, as was the news that Special Forces were now operating in Afghanistan (when most informed analysts believed this had started some four weeks ago).

The US Rangers attack near Kandahar on 19–20 October was initially represented as the successful clearing of a previously impregnable Taliban stronghold, but further information indicated that the target area had few troops there, and the operation was essentially a 'dry run' for further attacks, ensuring that the complicated logistics for this kind of operation could work in practice.

One of the problems for media handlers is that the media itself expects a constant 'feed' of stories, made more necessary because it cannot get its own people into the war zone. Yet Bush, Rumsfeld and others have constantly emphasised that they are engaged in a potentially long war. To avoid a rise in media criticism of the war, we should therefore expect a continual string of 'hardware' stories in the coming weeks and months.

Iraq and Israel

In the past week there have been no significant developments in relation to Iraq. US hard-line defence advisers still want the war to be taken to Iraq but are not yet succeeding, and may not do so. Iraq, meanwhile, is not providing any provocation, but has successfully rebuilt the command and control systems that were damaged in extensive US air attacks last February.

US and EU efforts to encourage an Israeli-Palestinian cease-fire have been hugely damaged by the Zee'vi assassination and the consequent Israeli military response. The al-Qaida network has not focused much attention on the Palestinian cause, being mainly concerned with US 'occupation' of the Gulf and the illegitimacy of the Saudi regime, but any harsh Israeli military action strengthens the network's support in the region (and that for Iraq, too).

US and al-Qaida strategy

The US strategy is one of hugely damaging the Taliban regime, causing its collapse and making anti-al-Qaida interventions much more feasible. Given the massive military capabilities of the United States, it ought to be possible to overthrow the Taliban regime, but there are two doubts. The first is that more bombing may actually increase support for the regime. Previous large-scale bombings by the former Soviet Union in the 1980s, some of them killing 5,000 or more people in individual cities, tended to increase opposition to their intervention. This could happen again, even if the Taliban has limited popular support. The second is that there really is a huge humanitarian crisis developing, and this is almost certain to rise up the political agenda in the coming weeks.

The more difficult part of the analysis is understanding the al-Qaida strategy. Given that it appears to form part of a loose coalition of networks spread over a number of countries, and that this coalition has been developing and has been involved in paramilitary action for ten years, it is best to assume that it is currently operating on a five- to ten-year strategy.

As such, many of its elements may well have dispersed, not just throughout Afghanistan but into a number of other countries, and it may be intending to remain in a dispersed form for many months if not two or three years. As such, when US ground forces progressively seek to destroy the network before and after the coming winter, it may simply not be around to be destroyed. Meanwhile, a destructive conflict will further damage Afghanistan, already suffering the effects of a three-year drought and 20 years of war.

The horizon of war lengthens
5 November 2001

There have been bombing raids on targets in Afghanistan for 29 days, and the past week has seen two significant changes – a move to area bombing and to economic targeting. The first has involved the use of small numbers of B-52 strategic bombers engaged in area attacks on presumed Taliban military concentrations close to areas of Northern Alliance activity. The B-52 is the largest bomber in service anywhere in the world, and was used extensively in Vietnam and more recently in Iraq for area bombing.

The aim in the current conflict appears to be to weaken Taliban positions, allowing a more successful advance by Northern Alliance forces. These have been strengthened by new arms supplies coming from Russia (reportedly paid for by the US), with further supplies on the way. There are also reported to be more US forces working with the Northern Alliance, and the probable availability of bases in Tajikistan will enhance these deployments.

At the same time, the use of the B-52s remains on a small scale, partly because of the distances involved in flying from Diego Garcia, and partly because of the limited deployment space at that base. Furthermore, there are almost certainly only a few areas in which Taliban forces are at all concentrated. Also, some of the areas involved are honeycombed with underground irrigation tunnels – not mapped, not visible to satellites, but known to local people. These provide shelter and transit routes to Taliban forces that are, in any case, widely dispersed. These 'front lines' are themselves fluid and inter-mingled with small farms and villages, so that any kind of area bombing is likely to cause civilian casualties.

In any case, it seems unlikely that the Northern Alliance is in a position to make any significant advance on Kabul before winter sets in, unless it gets immediate and very substantial additional aid from the United States. What is more likely is that an effort is made to dislodge Taliban forces from their more isolated location in the northern city of Mazar-e-Sharif. Even this is not very likely without the close involvement of US forces, either as large numbers of advisers or as combat troops. The recent Northern Alliance attempt to advance on the city was repulsed with serious casualties. Taking the city would provide a base within Afghanistan for military operations and for relief convoys, although the mixing of these two very different activities is, at best, a dubious process.

A reprise of economic targeting

The second development, hardly reported in the media, has been the attacks on power supplies, especially a hydroelectric power station near Kandahar. While such targeting has been predicted, and may well have some effect on Taliban capabilities, its main effect will be on the well-being of civilians, especially as winter approaches. It certainly fits a pattern common to recent US use of air power. The war on Iraq involved sustained economic targeting, and this was also employed against Serbia when military targets proved so difficult to find (from 15,000 feet). In that case, US economic targeting did some $60 billion worth of damage to the Serbian economy in a few weeks. Such tactics against Afghanistan, one of the poorest countries in the world, will not have that economic effect, but will certainly exact a human cost, whatever its effects on the Taliban.

Much of the action in Afghanistan is currently involving attempts to increase support for opposition groups in a number of parts of the country, although success is so far limited. There are also a number of Special Operations units being employed, some of them inserted and extracted by helicopter. There are only a few sketchy reports of these activities, but some suggest an unexpectedly high level of opposition when these units actually engage with Taliban forces. Reports circulating in the Gulf states suggest that there have been casualties among some Special Forces units, but these remain completely unconfirmed.

Overall, more than four weeks of bombing appears to have had very little effect in diminishing the power of the Taliban regime, and there are some indications of increasing support for the regime within Afghanistan, or at least for opposition to US action. There appears to have been almost no effective action taken against al-Qaida forces, and it is not clear whether these remain in any coherent form in Afghanistan. There is every probability that they are already well dispersed, both inside and outside the country.

Winter conditions make normal transport and communications difficult for the highland areas of Afghanistan, and existing food shortages make major humanitarian problems highly likely. The situation remains very fluid, and might just involve sudden and rapid change, but it looks probable that the most significant 'advance' by the US will be the very limited objective of securing Mazar-e-Sharif, and attempting to move on from there to limit and ultimately overthrow the Taliban regime.

No early resolution

Apart from many uncertainties, there are two problems with this. The first is that the Northern Alliance remains, at best, unstable, and also unrepresentative of Afghanistan as a whole. The second is that arms are now flooding into Northern Alliance areas, and will cascade through the country in the coming months and years, making further conflict more costly.

In the wider region, opposition to the war is growing, and is complicated by the increasing intransigence of the Sharon government in Israel, including his refusal to travel to Washington this week. Mr Blair, to his credit, has recognised the crucial importance of improving Israeli-Palestinian relations, but the reaction to his recent visit has shown how far the divisions go.

In the United States, Mr Bush's standing has taken a knock with the anthrax problems but domestic support for the war is remarkably solid, and looks likely to remain so. Outside of the few quality broadsheets, some magazines and a few specialist broadcasting outlets, there is little coverage of the more problematic aspects of the war.

Looked at overall, threats against the Taliban delivered before the bombing commenced had been expected to encourage them to give up bin Laden and key parts of the al-Qaida network. That did not happen. Then the bombing was expected to cause a Taliban collapse. That has not yet happened. It would appear that the most that might be expected before winter will be the taking of one Afghan city and the establishment of forward bases for further military action. Perhaps there will be a sudden Taliban collapse, but it seems unlikely. A long war is in prospect, with all the human costs involved.

The Taliban factor
13 November 2001

Two months after the New York and Washington attacks, the sixth week of the war, there have been substantial developments that make it a little easier to analyse the direction, possible duration and likely effects of the war. These partly relate to the mood in the United States, but also concern the recent and rapid Taliban withdrawal from much of northern Afghanistan, including Kabul.

The American mood

Although the Bush administration has found it difficult to handle the anthrax attacks, support for the war itself is remarkably strong. Away from the public service broadcasting channels and a few of the more heavyweight broadsheets, the culture is one of 'America Strikes Back'. This comes through strongly and persistently on all of the major TV news bulletins, with little or no critical analysis.

In one sense, this accurately reflects the public mood, although there is a certain underlying concern about the uncertainties of the war, and a much greater unease arising from a sense of vulnerability within the United States itself. 11 September does really only compare with Pearl Harbor, except that in 1941 there was a clearly defined state as the palpable enemy. 'Terrorism' has become the pseudo-state, with the Taliban and bin Laden expressed as the embodiment of that near-virtual enemy.

As a consequence, the destruction of the Taliban has become the dominant war aim, at least in the short term, and almost anything goes in its pursuit, including an uncomfortable public debate on the possible use of physical interrogation (torture). There is very little general concern about civilian casualties. The Secretary of Defense, Donald Rumsfeld, was casually dismissive of such losses in an interview last week; he acknowledged only that there might have been three or four civilians killed in one case, but implied that any talk of serious casualties was Taliban propaganda. We are not quite at the 'gook count' attitude of Vietnam days, but not far from it.

There is, significantly, a widespread acceptance that the Afghanistan War could be costly for US troops. A *USA Today*/CNN/Gallup poll published on 8 November found that nearly half those polled would accept more than 10,000 casualties among US forces. The same poll indicated that 55 per cent would back a war lasting more than two years.

Public opinion can be fickle, and views might change rapidly if the war drags on through the winter and substantial US casualties eventually ensue during counter-guerrilla conflicts in the Taliban-controlled areas. Even so, it is worth appreciating that the loss of those two World Trade Center towers, the most notable buildings in post-war America, has struck deep. This is reflected in the ease with which the administration has pushed through an immediate 10 per cent increase in defence spending, with many members of Congress arguing that this is too little.

The proposed increase, $32.3 billion, is about the same as Britain's *entire* annual defence budget, and includes $5.5 billion for additional munitions and $4.5 billion for force protection. The latter is an indication of the perception that US forces overseas are going to face increased threats to their security, especially in the Middle East and South-west Asia, as the war drags on. The new budget also includes repairs to the Pentagon, now estimated at $500 million. In addition, the navy, in particular, is already running down its stocks of laser-guided bombs and Tomahawk cruise missiles, and priority will be given to replacing these and similar weapons.

Retreat from Mazar-e-Sharif and Kabul

Meanwhile, in Afghanistan, the speed of the advance of the Northern Alliance across the north of Afghanistan, including the taking of Mazar-e-Sharif and the Taliban withdrawal from Kabul, has been a surprise to virtually every analyst. There are three factors involved in this change of circumstance, although they do not sufficiently explain these rapid developments.

Firstly, from around 4 November, the US substantially escalated its air attacks on Taliban positions, with much heavier use of area bombing by B-52s. The capacity of these planes is considerable. The standard munition used recently in area bombing is the unguided 250 kg bomb. Each bomb has about twice the destructive power of each of the Provisional IRA bombs that did so much damage to the centre of Manchester, and the Baltic Exchange, Bishopsgate and Canary Wharf districts of London during the mid-1990s.

Each B-52 can deliver more than 50 of these bombs in a single attack. Used extensively, and targeted by US Special Forces working in co-ordination with Northern Alliance troop movements, the effects have been considerable. Given that Taliban concentrations have been inter-spersed with local people in villages and smallholdings, the 'colateral damage' (i.e. people killed) will also have been considerable. This is unlikely to be acknowledged, certainly not by Mr Rumsfeld.

The second factor is that Northern Alliance forces have been sub-stantially armed from Russia, using American aid, enabling them to advance more quickly and constitute a more significant force. Thirdly, they have been advancing in areas in which the Taliban militia have largely been occupying forces, often controlling territory that has only been in their possession for two to three years.

Even so, these factors do not sufficiently explain the manner in which the war has changed, with large-scale advances by the Northern Alliance seeming even to indicate the rapid fall of the Taliban regime.

What next?

There are two possible explanations, and whichever is more accurate will largely determine the nature of the next part of the war. One expla-nation is that the Taliban militia are so incompetent and lacking in support that they can offer little real resistance in the face of a rather mediocre Northern Alliance backed up by substantial air power.

If this is correct, then Jalalabad and Kandahar will fall quickly, and the Taliban regime will lose control over all but small pockets of Afghanistan. US and other forces will move in rapidly to bases in the country in the coming few weeks and the al-Qaida network will be destroyed in the next few months.

Afghanistan may then be controlled by a Northern Alliance that is composed largely of warlord groups with an appalling human rights record, the al-Qaida network may be largely dispersed to other locations, perhaps in a position to prepare for further paramilitary action. But this phase of the war on terrorism will be considered to have been 'won'.

The alternative explanation is that the experience of area bombing and of fighting a re-equipped Northern Alliance working closely with US forces may have convinced Taliban military leaders that they cannot win a war fought primarily on US terms. This may be especially so as the United States becomes increasingly able to operate from bases in Uzbekistan and Tajikistan, as well as within Northern Afghanistan itself.

On this basis, it would make little sense for the Taliban to try and maintain control of areas outside of its natural Pashtun support zone. Better, rather, to withdraw to its numerous local power bases in central and southern Afghanistan, allow the Northern Alliance to extend *their* areas of operations outside their zones of support, and engage in guerrilla warfare, even if this means withdrawing from Kandahar as well as Kabul.

In looking at this second possibility, four things are worth noting. One is that previous experience of the Northern Alliance suggests that it is, at best, an unstable coalition, with every prospect of fracturing between the different factions as new territory is gained. It also includes elements capable of dreadful human rights abuses, and there are already reports of massacres after the taking of Mazar-e-Sharif.

The second is that Taliban militia proved to be militarily effective in driving the Northern Alliance warlords from most of Afghanistan just a few years ago. Thirdly, there have been unconfirmed but plausible reports that most of the key Taliban militia groups withdrew from Mazar-e-Sharif and the surrounding region some days before the Northern Alliance advance, a factor which would itself help to explain the speed of the latter's advance. It is certainly clear that the Taliban withdrawal from Kabul was both sudden and rapid, being undertaken overnight to limit the capacity of US strike aircraft to attack the forces on the road.

Finally, there is always a tendency to analyse a conflict through western eyes, so that the capture of cities such as Kabul, Jalalabad and Kandahar would tend to lead to the conclusion that the Taliban was defeated and the war was over. But Afghanistan is a very poor country that is not greatly urbanised. Most of the population remains spread over towns, villages, farms and smallholdings throughout the lowlands and, to an extent, the highlands of the Hindu Kush and elsewhere.

It would therefore be perfectly possible for the Taliban to withdraw to their Pashtun heartlands, forming small groups scattered through extensive rural communities and able to offer continual opposition, largely through guerrilla warfare, to Northern Alliance forces.

The Taliban factor

Whether this happens depends on one aspect which remains unclear – the extent of support for the Taliban in the Pashtun areas of Afghanistan. This is why the CIA has put so much effort into helping anti-Taliban figures such as Hamid Karzai. If such people can unite Pashtun elements against the Taliban, then their position would be greatly weakened, but there are several reasons to question this.

For a start, there are reports that members of the Pakistan Intelligence Service have been supplying Taliban units with useable weapons. Furthermore, support for the Taliban remains high in north-western parts of Pakistan, with thousands of volunteers available for service. Perhaps most significant is that the people of the Pashtun areas of Afghanistan, whatever their attitude towards the Taliban, may see the Northern Alliance and the United States as a single entity, taking a quasi-nationalist stand against what are seen to be 'foreign' occupying forces.

When the Taliban first became prominent in Afghanistan in the mid-1990s, they became popular in Pashtun areas, not least because of the brutal behaviour of the warlord forces that later came to make up much of the Northern Alliance. Furthermore, there is a certain anti-

American sentiment that has been greatly exacerbated by recent proselytising. Northern Alliance advances into Pashtun areas made possible by repeated US bombing could serve mainly to provide communal support for Taliban and allied militias in the Pashtun areas of Afghanistan. If so, effective resistance could be protracted and US efforts to identify al-Qaida units and bases made much more difficult.

Many of these questions will be answered in the next month or so, but it would be very unwise to assume that the war is close to an end. Even so, the Bush administration retains great domestic support, it has the capability to use immensely strong military force, and based on previous US performance in Serbia, Somalia and Iraq, will certainly do so. Thus, the bombing continues, arms pour into northern Afghanistan and, at the very least, many ordinary people will get caught up in the conflict and will be killed, maimed or succumb to malnutrition and disease. As in so many recent wars 'the young men do the fighting – the rest do the dying'.

Breakthrough – to a broader war?
19 November 2001

Over the period 8–13 November, there was a radical change in the war in Afghanistan, with the Taliban retreating throughout the majority of the areas under their control. A week ago, there appeared to be three reasons for this. One was the intensity of the US bombing of Taliban positions (probably with numerous civilian casualties). A second was the equipping of the Northern Alliance with substantial armaments, provided by Russia but substantially financed by the United States. Finally the Taliban leaders appeared determined to withdraw from non-Pashtun areas, some of which had only been occupied by them for a couple of years.

On the basis of this probable analysis, and bearing in mind that the withdrawal from Kabul had been sufficiently efficient to minimise US air attacks on retreating forces, it looked likely that the Taliban intended to retreat to more dispersed rural areas that would be less amenable to air attack. An alternative view was that an almost total Taliban defeat was imminent.

Towards the end of the seventh week of the war, the latter view looked more likely, and it was expected that the remaining Taliban city of Kandahar would quickly be vacated, and that the isolated group holding on to Kunduz in the north would soon surrender.

Given that the United States will now concentrate a very heavy bombing campaign on these two target areas, it is probable that both will soon fall. In the process, and given the nature of the bombing, substantial civilian casualties are likely.

At the same time, the expected collapse of all significant Taliban groups has not yet happened and the unity of the Northern Alliance is questionable. While there is a general view that the war is close to its end, this is by no means certain. Furthermore, the experience of the last two weeks raises a range of relevant issues.

The US/Northern Alliance coalition

Some three weeks into the war, the area bombing of Taliban forward positions was greatly intensified, and this was accompanied by a rapid rearming of the Northern Alliance and the insertion of Special Forces to assist their advance. This amounted to a tacit policy of utilising the Northern Alliance as the ground troops against the Taliban regime, even though the Northern Alliance was of dubious stability and had elements with appalling human rights records.

The reason for the Bush administration's decision to take this 'short cut' to attempt the defeat of the Taliban was almost certainly the great difficulty that would be involved in getting substantial US ground forces into the region, and the consequent likelihood that the war would continue through next year.

In the event, this military policy had its effect much earlier than had been anticipated, with the result that much of Afghanistan is now controlled by a range of warlords and factions, with a united and representative government rather difficult to envisage. It would be grossly unfair to blame those United Nations officials now trying to facilitate just such a government if they find themselves unable to do so – their task is difficult in the extreme.

It should also be expected that the United States itself will not have any great interest in the immediate future government of Afghanistan, even though its military strategy has been responsible for the current state of affairs. It will be much more concerned with further action against the Taliban and the al-Qaida network.

The intensity of the bombing

The US bombing strategy intensified dramatically at the beginning of November, and by 18 November about 13,500 tons of ordnance had been used in the war, the great majority of it being unguided bombs dropped by B-52 and B-1B bombers in the past three weeks.

Particular use was made of the BLU-82 fuel-air bomb, a weapon originally developed during the Vietnam War. Although only two were used against Taliban positions around Mazar-e-Sharif, their effect was devastating.

The BLU-82 contains 12,600 lb of a mixture of ammonium nitrate and aluminium powder with a polystyrene soap binder. This disperses as a highly volatile fuel which is detonated to produce an effect equivalent to 30 tons of TNT. It is indiscriminate in its effect and is the largest bomb ever used in conventional warfare.

Russia's position

One of the most remarkable beneficiaries of the last two weeks has been President Putin's Russia. Having long supported the Northern Alliance, it now finds itself arming the troops (with US funding) and advising and supporting the recent advances. There are indications that forces from Uzbekistan and possibly Tajikistan actually fought alongside Northern Alliance troops during the recent advances, a tactic that would only have been agreed by their respective governments with 'approval' from Moscow, given the influence of Russia in both states.

For the first time since the end of the Cold War, Russia now has considerable influence in Afghanistan, a substantial and unexpected bonus provided largely by the United States. Furthermore, its continuing support for the Northern Alliance allies it with groups of warlords while, at the same time, its own behaviour in Chechnya is unlikely to be subject to criticism from Washington.

US judicial developments

Two aspects of the domestic actions of the Bush administration are worth noting at this stage. The first is that large numbers of people of Middle Eastern origin have been detained in the United States. The total figure exceeds 1,000, and it has not always proved easy for their legal representatives to perform their professional functions effectively.

Related to this is the recent presidential directive that military courts be enabled to try those suspected of paramilitary activities. This directive, issued on 13 November, was reported to be the first since the Second World War. Such courts could convene in the United States or overseas, including in Afghanistan, and it would be within the power of Mr Bush to determine who should be so tried.

The trials could be held in private, would not need to involve juries and could give sentences up to and including life imprisonment or the death penalty. A White House spokesperson described the presidential order as 'an additional tool to use as he sees fit to fight the war on terrorism and bring foreign terrorists to justice'.

The United States currently retains its objections to the establishment of a broadly based International Criminal Court.

Iraq

The pursuit of the al-Qaida network may still take weeks or months, and it is certainly possible that Afghanistan may be entering a new phase in its interminable civil war, but the view from Washington is that the achievements of the past two weeks have been little short of spectacular. Given the hard-line nature of President Bush's international security community (with just a few exceptions) it is highly likely that more attention will now be given to the possibility of taking action against the regime of Saddam Hussein in Baghdad.

This may not develop rapidly, and it is just possible that a coalition involving Russia, France and some regional states may be assembled to put indirect pressure on the regime. More likely is the development of plans for military action, with these primarily focusing on substantial and persistent air attacks to cripple the regime. While there would be serious misgivings in many European and Middle Eastern states, there would be very substantial domestic political support for such a policy.

Israel

The Bush administration is clearly aware of the dangers posed by the government of Mr Sharon in Israel, and would want to maintain pressure on Mr Sharon to re-open meaningful negotiations with the

Palestinians. It is also worth remembering that it was in the aftermath of the Gulf War that the previous Bush administration recognised the need for movement on this front.

At the same time, the Sharon government is markedly extreme in its outlook and policies. It is therefore likely to see the events of the past two weeks as reducing the pressure that it was under to limit its action against Palestinian elements. As a consequence, it might be well to expect an escalation of the levels of violence in the occupied territories. The recent difficult reception afforded to a high level team from the European Union is an indicator of current Israeli government opinion.

Al-Qaida

There is an assumption that the al-Qaida network has been hugely damaged by the recent Taliban collapse. This may be true, but only to a certain extent. It should be recalled that the network appears to be part of a coalition of groups stretching over many countries and drawing primarily on supporters in the western Gulf states and North Africa. It may also be the case that many key elements of the network have long since left Afghanistan.

It is likely that elements of the network, or other groups loosely associated with it, still have the capacity for further attacks such as those of 11 September. If so, the US action in Afghanistan may prompt such attacks in the near future.

In search of enemies
27 November 2001

A more complicated conflict with unexpected consequences

Following the retreat of substantial Taliban forces from most of northern Afghanistan in the period 8–13 November, there was an expectation that the entire Taliban force would collapse relatively quickly. This was not a universally shared view, and an alternative analysis was that the withdrawal was at least partly strategic. By the end of the sixth week of the war, there appeared to be some support for the latter view, with Taliban forces still in control of Kunduz, and little sign of a collapse around Kandahar and in the four provinces still under Taliban control.

For most of the seventh week, the Taliban forces remained in Kunduz, with a progressive surrender or withdrawal only becoming apparent at the end of the week. Even then, some Taliban forces that had surrendered and had been moved to Mazar-e-Sharif, broke out of their camp and engaged local warlord forces with substantial loss of life, especially after the intervention of US strike aircraft. Furthermore, there had earlier been a short period of unexpected Taliban resistance close to Kabul itself.

These events all indicated that, in some circumstances, Taliban and associated forces might offer resistance, both to forces of the Northern Alliance (= United Front) or to other warlord groups or non-Taliban elements from the Pashtun areas. At the very least, the situation had become more complex.

In the southern Taliban-controlled provinces there seemed little sign that Northern Alliance forces, or their associates, would seek confrontation. Further inroads into Taliban areas of control would seem more likely only as a result of very intensive US air action, combined with US use of Special Forces and regular ground troops. The landing of a fairly substantial force of US Marines at Kandahar Airport on 25 November, and the subsequent establishment of a ground base, indicates that such a posture might now be under development.

There are indications that most Taliban forces have already withdrawn from Kandahar. While the United States may spend some days in building up its base near the city, the takeover of the city by local anti-Taliban forces (not Northern Alliance forces) may be rapid. This does not imply the end of the Taliban, with many already ensconced in well-armed locations in villages or in mountainous areas.

The United States and the Northern Alliance

In the past week it has become more clear that the US has been single-minded in its decision to work closely with the Northern Alliance elsewhere in Afghanistan, with substantial military advice being offered on the ground, a comprehensive rearming process under way (largely from Russia) and much closer and more intensive use of air strikes.

At the same time, the anticipated cracks in Northern Alliance solidarity are becoming more obvious, and there are indications that substantial parts of Afghanistan are not under a united Northern Alliance control and have reverted to what amounts to warlord control. Even within the Northern Alliance itself, divisions are extending to something approaching 'warlordism'.

This process of fragmentation, a local version of 'Balkanisation', will clearly make it more difficult for the UN and other agencies to help foster a united, broad-based Afghan polity. And it has three further likely consequences – for drug production, arms importation and legal order.

First, those areas under essentially local control, which are also suitable for growing opium poppies, are likely to see a substantial expansion in cultivation. Areas long controlled by the Northern Alliance were already witnessing a substantial increase in opium production, in contrast to the temporary cessation in Taliban areas. Some recent US air strikes have been directed at opium-processing facilities, but these will have only a short-term impact, as the lucrative trade will simply devolve to smaller, dispersed units.

The loss of Taliban control has resulted in previously hidden stocks appearing in Pakistan. These are likely to herald a substantial improvement in availability, bringing the price down in the major markets, especially Europe. Thus, one effect of US co-operation with the Northern Alliance, aside from the use of US ground troops to defeat the Taliban, will be substantially increased opium production in Afghanistan. This is virtually inevitable as local warlords seek sources of income to maintain their position and poor people seek their own sources of income at a time of serious food shortages.

Second, in recent weeks wide ranges of arms have flooded into northern Afghanistan from Russia, and will cascade throughout much of the country. This will greatly aid the third factor, the partial breakdown of law enforcement and order.

Law, order and the Taliban

In the last two to three years, the Taliban regime became intensely unpopular in much of Afghanistan, not least because of its theological rigidity, its attitude to women, its use of barbaric punishments and the often brutal suppression of dissent. At the same time, it is relevant to remember that the Taliban regime was initially welcomed as it gained control of much of the country because of the manner in which it dealt with warlords and banditry.

In other words, the Taliban imposed law (of a sort) and order on much of the country, after several years of disorder verging on chaos. As the Taliban has withdrawn, that form of repressive order has been replaced by widespread disorder that has already cost the lives of a number of foreign journalists and, no doubt, of many local people. It is a disorder made more dangerous by the almost universal availability of firearms, there is little prospect of the Northern Alliance imposing any systematic semblance of order, and there is little or no indication of US interest in doing so.

One effect of this situation is to make the local delivery of aid shipments highly problematic. A number of agencies are reporting that it is easier to get shipments into central locations in Afghanistan, but much more difficult to distribute them to the areas in need because of banditry, looting and related problems.

In short, the US–Northern Alliance combination has successfully diminished Taliban control and has probably already damaged those elements of the al-Qaida network still present in Afghanistan (although most may have long since left). There has thus been progress in the two primary war aims of the United States.

At the same time, a parallel result has been disorder in much of the country, increasing factionalism, greater difficulties in distributing much-needed aid at a time of severe food shortages, and the likelihood of a substantial increase in heroin production for European markets.

The end of US unilateralism?

One of the expected consequences of the 11 September atrocities was that the United States administration would see the need for much closer international co-operation in the pursuit of its security needs. Prior to 11 September, the Bush administration had shown a strong unilateralist orientation, including opposition to the Comprehensive Test Ban Treaty (CTBT), to planned negotiations on the control of the militarisation of space and to the proposed international criminal court. There were disagreements on the land mine ban, on UN proposals for the control of light arms transfers and on the continuation of the Anti-Ballistic Missile Treaty, and opposition to the

protocol designed to strengthen the biological weapons convention.
Most notably, there was a withdrawal from the Kyoto climate change
protocols.

After an initial period in which it appeared that the trauma of 11
September would occasion a change of attitude, it now looks as if
unilateralism is alive and kicking, and expressing itself in a number
of ways. For example, the US did not even bother with representa-
tion at recent CTBT discussions, and its statement at the biological
weapons talks in Geneva was notably hard-line. There were no indications of any willingness to change its attitude to the protocol that
has been negotiated with painful difficulty over the past six years.
Given that this protocol has attracted support from many states,
including strong support in Europe, this is especially unfortunate.

More specifically, the United States has taken concrete steps in
two other directions. One, mentioned in the previous article, is the
presidential directive that military courts be allowed to try suspected
terrorists. The status of such prisoners would be determined by the
president, with courts able to meet in secret, and overseas, and able
to give sentences up to and including life imprisonment and the
death penalty. This directive has caused some consternation among
constitutional and international lawyers in the US, but is unlikely to
be withdrawn.

The second issue concerns changed rules of operation for the CIA,
removing a number of restrictions on modes of action originally put
in place at the time of the Carter administration. The CIA's Special
Operations Division, with its history of covert operations, coup
support and targeted assassinations, is likely to become a key element
in President Bush's 'war on terrorism'. In one sense, this represents
a return to the days of the Cold War, except that the 'enemy' is far
less clear-cut than communist insurgents and their Soviet backers.
Indeed, the 'enemy' may have a far wider definition, taking in a
wide rage of groups that appear to oppose US interests.

Extending the war

Although the future direction of the war in Afghanistan remains
uncertain, there has been sufficient movement for there to be an
indication of plans to extend the war to other states that are perceived
to be harbouring groups associated with al-Qaida. These include,

variously, Yemen, Somalia and Sudan. In the longer term, the more hard-line international security advisers in Washington remain absolutely convinced of the necessity of destroying the Saddam Hussein regime in Iraq, possibly by encouraging Kurdish and Shi'ite rebellions accompanied by an intensive and protracted bombing campaign against the Iraqi armed forces and their support systems.

Given the attitude of the administration and its long-term commitment to its war on terrorism, media speculation of an extension of the war should not be surprising. In view of the remarkable US military superiority in relation to any other state, let alone some of the poorest countries on earth, US action should certainly be possible.

There is, though, a note of caution. The United States administration still has a concern over casualties among its own troops and will therefore base future action primarily on air strikes. But the air war against the Taliban and al-Qaida has already used up precision-guided munitions at an extraordinary rate, so much so that there has had to be an emergency airlift of stocks from bases in Kuwait that would ordinarily be used for actions against Iraq.

US defence companies are already moving to 'surge production' of such munitions, a singularly profitable endeavour, but it will take some time to build up stocks for further major military action in countries other than Afghanistan. Furthermore, the movement of ground troops around southern Afghanistan, now that a base has been established at Kandahar, will involve considerable air support, including the frequent use of precision-guided munitions.

In short, the rapid changes of the last two weeks have raised the possibility that the war is nearly over. This is not the view of military planners in Washington. Lengthy operations in Afghanistan going on over the winter are still, on balance, more likely. The extension of the war to other parts of the world will be a longer-term process. Indeed, in all probability, the 'war on terrorism' will occupy most of the rest of President Bush's first administration, extending into his anticipated second term.

2
War in Afghanistan – II

During the course of December 2001, the war in Afghanistan appeared to come to a fairly rapid end. The last major population centres under Taliban control fell to the Northern Alliance or other warlords, and there was an assumption that al-Qaida had been hugely damaged. Certainly, the hold over much of Afghanistan by regional warlords was already beginning to become apparent, as was the 'cascading' of large numbers of weapons into and through the country. The war itself was being shown to be causing substantial casualties, with perhaps 3,000 or more civilians killed – similar to the numbers killed in New York and Washington three months earlier.

More evidence was emerging of the manner in which Taliban militia appeared able to 'melt away' from areas of heavy fighting, most notably in their extraordinary overnight withdrawal from Kabul. It appeared more and more likely that there was a near-country-wide tactic of withdrawing, wherever the combination of US air attacks and Northern Alliance ground forces meant that resistance was pointless. A consequence of this was that Taliban units still had a capacity to engage in guerrilla warfare, a capacity that would become more significant in the following six months.

Even as the war in Afghanistan was proceeding in a manner satisfying to Washington, there was a prescient warning from the British Chief of the Defence Staff that such success did not mean a wider victory in the 'war on terror'. Such a warning appeared to have little effect on attitudes in Washington, even though it was becoming clear that Taliban and al-Qaida militia had little difficulty in moving between Afghanistan and Pakistan.

More generally, the US security agenda was developing along unilateral lines, not least with the opposition to any strengthening of the Biological and Toxin Weapons Convention. Although little noticed in the western press at the time, the effective wrecking of over six years of painstaking negotiations in Geneva caused considerable anger among diplomats and experts in Western Europe and the wider world, and was one of the factors that began to lead to a rift in the transatlantic relations.

Afghanistan: victory or swamp?
4 December 2001

By the end of the eighth week of the war, there was an expectation that, with the imminent occupation of Kunduz, the southern Taliban city of Kandahar would quickly fall. It was thought that this was made more likely by the establishment of a substantial forward operating base by the US Marines at an airstrip in the desert well to the south of Kandahar.

Latest developments

During the past week there have been two significant developments, both of which point to the future direction of the war. The first is that the United States has extended its policy of using local militia as ground troops with the US providing air power and Special Operations Forces and substantial quantities of arms and other equipment.

The speed of the Taliban withdrawal from Northern Afghanistan was partly caused by the rapid arming of Northern Alliance forces, with arms coming from Russia but largely paid for by the US. In the south of the country there appeared to be little prospect of Northern Alliance militia moving into Pashtun areas, and, as a result, there has been a substantial arming of anti-Taliban Pashtun groups. It is these that have been advancing slowly towards Kandahar, with heavy US bombing aiming to kill Taliban troops and encourage others to defect.

In essence, the overall US policy has been to take sides in the long-lasting civil war, supporting any groups opposed to the Taliban, whatever their own record of violence and human rights abuses. One of the longer-term effects of this will be to leave a country that has been flooded with arms, with these likely to be disseminated among the population. The United Nations has some of its best career diplomats engaged in trying to establish an acceptable unified government, but even short-term progress in this direction may quickly be undone in the coming months by local and regional violence.

The second development of the past week has been the manner in which many Taliban units have been treated. There have now been repeated instances of prisoners being summarily executed, with, in addition, the killing of several hundred Taliban at the fort at Mazar-e-Sharif. While some kind of revolt may have taken place, it is also clear that the intensity of the counter-attack meant that there would be few survivors. Furthermore, many of those killed still had their hands tied behind their backs.

No one is pretending that the Taliban had any particular regard for human rights – their treatment of opponents over the past six years has frequently been brutal in the extreme. At the same time, though, the treatment meted out to them cannot be blamed merely on Northern Alliance militia seeking reprisals. The point is that the United States has formed a direct and close coalition with these groups rather than use its own ground troops. Furthermore, it was US firepower that was responsible for much of the killing at the fort.

A prolonged civil war?

A particularly significant aspect of this massacre is that it has been reported widely, and in detail, in the Middle East and South-west Asia. Some television footage of the aftermath of the killings has been shown on European channels, but most viewers have been spared the worst examples. This is not the case in the region, where satellite channels are reported to have described and screened the full extent of the carnage. This is likely to harden opinion against the United States and its associates, as well as serving to radicalise relatives and friends of those killed. It also makes it likely that those hard-line Taliban and al-Qaida supporters who do not change their allegiance will know that surrender is highly risky, motivating them to resist offensives by US forces and their associated local militia.

There has been an assumption, underlying much media analysis, that the fall of Kandahar would signal the impending end of the war. This is possible but unlikely. What seems more probable is that Taliban units will either melt away into villages, or take refuge in protected centres in the more mountainous regions. On this basis, there will be protracted operations in the coming weeks, and possible months, by US Special Forces and others, but these may not be able to isolate and attack all Taliban forces. Instead, there may be a tendency for these to avoid any encounters for many months, possibly entering into counter-movements against other Afghan forces next year.

Put bluntly, an apparent US victory achieved before the end of this year may, in reality, be just a further stage in a longer-term civil war in Afghanistan. This is supported by the likelihood that many Taliban and al-Qaida units have already crossed the border into north-west Pakistan, where there is substantial local support for their position, support no doubt fuelled by the recent treatment of Taliban prisoners.

Regional changes

The two main regional beneficiaries of the war so far have been Russia and India, and the main loser has been Pakistan. Russia has seen its influence increased in Tajikistan and Uzbekistan, it now has a virtual free hand to pursue its war in Chechnya with little or no condemnation from the United States, it has opened a diplomatic mission in Kabul in association with its long-time allies in the Northern Alliance and it has even succeeded in putting military forces into Bagram Air Base. Their purported mission – humanitarian support – does not seem to fit in with the heavy equipment they have brought with them.

India, too, has been a real beneficiary, giving strong support to the Northern Alliance and receiving notable support from the US Ambassador in Delhi in relation to its opposition to Islamic militia in Kashmir. Pakistan, on the other hand, now sees a potentially hostile state on both sides of its own territory, an outcome that is unlikely to aid the position of the current military regime, whatever its (rather unwilling) support for US action against al-Qaida.

Hidden developments

There have been some other significant developments that have largely escaped media attention.

Israel's military budget will run to nearly one-tenth of its gross domestic product next year, about three times that of the United States and four times the world average. A budget of $9.8 billion has been agreed for 2002, of which just over $2 billion is accounted for by US military aid.

The UK Ministry of Defence is reported to be considering the purchase of large numbers of land-attack Tomahawk cruise missiles.

Currently, Britain deploys Tomahawks on its nuclear-powered attack submarines. These are the Block IIIC missiles with a range of 1,000 miles and a 1,000 lb warhead, and another 48 of these are likely to be purchased, partly to replace missiles used recently. The new scheme would involved the purchase of up to 150 Block IV Tomahawks to equip the new Astute class of nuclear-powered submarines and possibly the new Type 45 destroyer. Tomahawks are considered to be particularly useful for fighting 'small wars in far-off places'.

President Bush's directive to allow people deemed to be terrorists to be tried in military tribunals operating in secret and capable of ordering the death sentence has run into some opposition in Congress. One senator, Patrick Leahy of Vermont, has said that the military order 'sends a message to the world that it is acceptable to hold secret trials and summary executions without the possibility of judicial review, at least when the defendant is a foreign national'. Meanwhile, the planning for the tribunals is going ahead, including the possibility of holding them at secure locations such as the west Pacific base on Guam or even on ships at sea.

The CIA and its activities in Afghanistan have both been subject to considerable criticism by sectors of the US armed forces. The general criticism was over its failure to recognise the extent of the threat from al-Qaida. The specific concern is with current CIA operations in Afghanistan where 'the Company' is said to be pursuing its own war, intent on making progress in order to counter the overall failure. As a result of this persistence, relations between the CIA and regional military commanders have come under stress, with the latter criticising the CIA for failing to share intelligence.

According to the well-informed journal *Aviation Week*, the CIA 'is being very aggressive and acting independently in the Central Asian theatre, say US officials who produce or control some of the key intelligence-gathering technologies being brought into play in Afghanistan'. One official told the journal that the CIA

have decided not to be just information gatherers. Now they're pulling the trigger on things – either directly or through Special Forces. But this is disruptive to any kind of co-ordination, it creates animosities between the CIA and the Defense Dept. because they're now competing with one another. The chase [of al-Qaida and Taliban leadership] is absolutely not being co-ordinated.

Given that this 'chase' is central to the conduct of the entire US action in Afghanistan, it is remarkable that there are the makings of a war within a war between different parts of the US intelligence and military forces.

The wages of war
10 December 2001

The last major centre of Taliban power, Kandahar, finally fell to a heterogeneous grouping of local anti-Taliban Pashtun militia at the end of last week. The US military policy of using local militia as ground forces has persisted, in spite of the establishment of a sizeable base some 50 miles from Kandahar occupied by elements of two Marine Expeditionary Units. There was some presumption that this base would serve as a point for an assault on Kandahar, but the US's sustained and heavy aerial bombardment has allowed it to maintain its policy.

In recent weeks, some 80 per cent of all US air strikes have been directed at Taliban front-line positions, especially around Kandahar, and the intensity of this attack was eventually sufficient to ensure the fall of the city. Even so, the manner of its surrender and the extent of casualties raise relevant questions.

With the fall of Kandahar, a pattern was maintained of Taliban surrendering to local militia, changing sides or, more commonly, simply melting away. Some foreign components of Taliban forces, probably in parallel with the more radical Taliban, have moved to more remote parts of southern and eastern Afghanistan, or else into Pakistan. In short, a continual feature of this war has been the near absence of sustained ground fighting, the exception being Kunduz, where Taliban units were surrounded by two elements of the Northern Alliance.

Instead, a fluid situation of multiple militia groups and local warlords exists in much of the country, roadblocks are frequent on the main highways, and there is an almost complete absence of any central authority. Progress at the UN-facilitated talks in Bonn was as good as could be expected, but much will hinge on whether it is possible to have some kind of temporary stabilisation force in the country. One problem is that the United States is not happy with this prospect, being concerned that the presence of disciplined and well-organised foreign troops will limit its capacity to range freely over the country in pursuit of al-Qaida and remaining Taliban leadership elements.

While much of the western media acts as though the war is well-nigh over, this is not the view in the Pentagon. There, the Marine Corps base near Kandahar is seen as the first step in a potentially protracted process involving persistent use of firepower provided by helicopter gunships, strike aircraft and heavy bombers. These forces will be ranged principally at remaining al-Qaida elements in Afghanistan, but also against Taliban groups.

Again, there is an assumption that virtually all Taliban activity has ceased. In practice, though, there has been continued resistance in areas near Kunduz, Kabul and Herat, and a substantial presence in north-west Afghanistan at Balkh near Mazar-e-Sharif, the latter involving over 2,000 Taliban and foreign forces.

Casualties

As the difficult task of identifying the casualties of the 11 September atrocities continues, the final number of people killed will be between 3,000 and 4,000. The casualties from the Afghanistan War are already likely to be well above that level, with many of them civilians. The extent of the casualties will be reasonably well known to the Pentagon. Bomb damage assessment (BDA) using satellites, drones and on-board cameras will all have given a wide-ranging view of the effects of the bombing, but little or nothing of this evidence will get into the public domain.

At the time of the Gulf War, much was made of precision bombing, but the reality was also the widespread and persistent use of carpet bombing and area impact munitions such as cluster bombs. In the immediate aftermath of the Gulf War, there were regional estimates of 70–100,000 Iraqis killed, but US government sources downplayed this, suggesting that the numbers were no more than a few thousand. More recently, as some independent assessments have been made, a figure far higher than that, of at least 20,000, seems more probable, with perhaps half of those being killed during the so-called 'turkey-shoot' attacks on the retreat from Kuwait.

Somewhat surprisingly, there have been some reasonably reliable indications of heavy civilian casualties already coming out of Afghanistan, with the *New York Times* last week quoting anti-Taliban pro-American commanders saying that hundreds of innocent villagers were being killed in the US bombing raids around Kandahar, Tora Bora and elsewhere. This appears to be an extension of the levels of casualties caused earlier in northern Afghanistan, when sustained US air attacks on Taliban positions did not distinguish between the Taliban and local villagers.

It is possible that reasonably reliable indications of the death toll may eventually be known, but this is not too likely. What is clear is that the US military posture has continued to be the very heavy use of bombing to support local militias. In such a war, substantial civilian casualties are inevitable but will not be admitted.

The first stage of a long war?

There are two major 'unknowns' at this stage of the war. One is the extent to which Taliban elements will go to ground for several months, seeking opportunities to regain power and influence if local militia continue their internal conflicts into next year. Much will depend on whether the UN and some key member states can make real progress in assisting the rebuilding of central political authority in Afghanistan, as well as the extent of US determination to continue seeking Taliban forces over the winter. The key point here is the manner in which the latter have simply melted away into the rural areas rather than, in most cases, surrendering, giving up their weapons and being taken prisoner.

Since they will have become inactive as militia, this will be considered part of a more general victory, but there is no way of knowing whether they will reassert themselves at a later date, especially if it proves difficult to establish a rule of law among rival local militias. This leaves Washington with the question of whether to maintain a military presence in Afghanistan that stretches over many months or possibly years.

The second question is the extent to which al-Qaida (and Taliban) groups have left Afghanistan for north-west Pakistan and elsewhere. The US participation in the Afghan civil war has effectively overturned the Taliban regime and has made it impossible for al-Qaida to maintain training bases there, at least in the short term, but the real problem remains as to whether this had been anticipated. Repeatedly over the last few weeks, attacks on al-Qaida camps, whether by US bombing or by occupation by local militia, have revealed an almost complete absence of al-Qaida members. They had already dispersed.

Again, it is worth taking the Pentagon view at face value – it is not always 'spin'. The word here is that a protracted process, stretching over some months, is still possible, with early indications of possible attacks on presumed bases in Somalia distinctly likely. What is more problematic for the United States is the likelihood of al-Qaida and Taliban elements remaining in north-west Pakistan. Also, and in addition to Somalia, there remains the desire in the Bush administration to extend the war to other areas of presumed paramilitary activity, including locations in Yemen and Lebanon, as well as the major potential adversary of Saddam Hussein's Iraq.

Regional considerations

Perhaps of more long-term significance than the recent fall of Kandahar were the suicide bombings in Israel, and the intensive and persistent Israeli response. In the light of the loss of life in Jerusalem and Haifa on 1–2 December, the Bush administration effectively gave Sharon a free hand to respond. This, combined with Arafat's weak leadership, is tending to strengthen the position of the more radical groups in the occupied territories, making the possibility of a more general Israeli-Palestinian war more likely, or even the development of an internal Palestinian civil conflict.

The US support for Israel is likely to be seen in much of the region as further evidence of its general anti-Arab and anti-Islamic policy. This is reinforced in the region by the Israeli use of US-built strike aircraft and attack helicopters in their repeated raids on the occupied territories, just as similar planes have been used intensively in Afghanistan over the past ten weeks.

In other words, US use of heavy air power in Afghanistan may appear in the west to have been a singular success, but it is highly dangerous to analyse matters purely through western eyes. The regional view is entirely different, and the combination of US action and a very hawkish Israeli government is actually more likely to establish a mood from which further radical movements will emerge.

It is worth remembering that persistent attempts by the Israelis to maintain control of the occupied territories by an 'iron fist' policy seem only to further radicalise their opponents, providing yet more potential martyrs for the cause.

US influence extended

Once again, some other indicators, largely missed by the media, are of interest. The first is that, according to *Jane's Defence Weekly*, the United States has established a temporary air base in Bulgaria, the first time that foreign troops have been stationed there since Soviet troops left in 1946. Six tanker aircraft will operate from Burgas Air Force Base in eastern Bulgaria for the duration of operations against Afghanistan, but this could establish an interesting precedent for operations in South-east Europe and South-west Asia, not least as a potential staging post for operations against Iraq.

Coupled with the US presence in Tajikistan, Uzbekistan, Pakistan and Afghanistan itself, it is an indication of how far the United States has been able to extend its military presence into the wider region, as a direct consequence of 11 September. Moreover, the extension of activities into Bulgaria has been done by the United States on its own, not as part of any NATO activity.

More cluster bombs

In another sign of the times, the Ministry of Defence in London is extending its arrangement with the defence manufacturer Insys to maintain supplies of the BL755 cluster bomb for RAF service, at least until 2006. The BL755 is one of the most widely deployed cluster weapons world-wide, over 50,000 having been manufactured for Britain and 16 overseas customers. Each cluster unit contains 147 'bomblets', each of which detonates to produce around 2,000 high-velocity shrapnel fragments.

Such cluster bombs are deployed principally against what are euphemistically termed 'soft targets'. As such they are devastating anti-personnel weapons and also act inadvertently as anti-personnel land mines when bomblets fail to explode. Human rights and anti-war groups have long campaigned to have them banned, but there is little sign of this. Most air forces regard these kinds of area impact munitions as useful for low- and medium-intensity operations. More than half of the 1,000-plus bombs dropped by the RAF in Kosovo and Serbia in 1999 were BL755 cluster bombs.

Combat proven

A feature of most recent conflicts has been the speed with which arms manufacturers advertise their latest products as 'combat proven'. Afghanistan is no exception, with Raytheon citing it in sales literature for its Joint Standoff Weapon (JSOW), a glide bomb with a range of over 40 miles, even as the war continues. 'Since 1999, JSOW has been combat proven in Operation Southern Watch, NATO Operation Allied Force and Operation Enduring Freedom ... .' JSOW comes in several variants, including sub-munitions for use against 'soft area targets' (e.g. people).

Bioweapon convention protocol stalled

Last week saw the end of the review conference on the 1972 Biological and Toxin Weapons Convention, following more than six years of negotiation to strengthen the treaty by bringing in an inspection regime. The protocol has been widely welcomed in Europe, with the UK playing a particularly active role. To widespread dismay, the United States delegation (led by John Bolton, the US Under-Secretary for Arms Control and International Security) waited until the last day of the discussions to announce that it remained opposed to the protocol, effectively wrecking any chance of getting it agreed in the near future. The whole matter has been put on ice for a year, but the US attitude, which has caused barely disguised frustration if not anger in European diplomatic circles, was a further indication of a distaste for multilateral arms control agreements that is well entrenched within the Bush administration.

The next frontier
17 December 2001

The bombing campaign and its implications

Until last Wednesday, local anti-Taliban militia had spent the best part of two weeks attempting to overcome a substantial force of al-Qaida and Taliban militia in the White Mountains area of south-east

Afghanistan. Towards the end of that period, US area bombing had been used to considerable effect, although it had also killed a number of anti-Taliban militia in 'friendly fire' incidents. US and UK Special Forces had operated alongside the militia, but largely in a target acquisition role.

By early last week, the effect of the bombing had been sufficient for anti-Taliban commanders to be able to negotiate a surrender deal with the Taliban/al-Qaida, an arrangement that was valuable to the former, not least in the context of their own casualties. However, the surrender would have involved a degree of safe passage for many of the militia and was firmly blocked by the United States. Instead, the bombing continued, on the basis of US and UK troops taking a much more active role in further fighting.

The extent of the bombing was remarkable. Prior to the air attacks around Tora Bora, US strategic air attacks throughout Afghanistan had used a range of carpet bombing techniques, together with the use of cluster bombs and, on three occasions, the dropping of the massive BLU-82 slurry bombs (erroneously termed 'daisy cutters' which refers to a type of fuse used on these and other bombs). According to the *Washington Post*, seven more of these bombs were dropped on Taliban/al-Qaida positions in rapid succession, along with repeated area bombing with conventional and cluster bombs, an intensity of bombardment that greatly exceeds anything seen elsewhere in Afghanistan in the past ten weeks.

Two things have become clear with these developments – one is the US war aim of minimising the possibilities of surrender of al-Qaida units, and the other is the extent to which air bombardment has underpinned so much of the war. Both of these are proving very effective in destroying those parts of the al-Qaida network still in Afghanistan, but the longer-term effects on the organisation, its wider coalitions and their widespread regional support are less clear. That there are concerns about the thrust of the overall campaign has become clear from a somewhat unexpected source.

A view from the centre

One of the most surprising events of the last week received far less attention than it deserved. This was the remarkably candid speech by Admiral Sir Michael Boyce, Britain's Chief of the Defence Staff

(CDS), on the current war and its possible long-term effects. The speech was given to an influential audience at the Royal United Services Institute in Whitehall, across the road from the War Office and Downing Street. In it, Boyce warned against the idea that a war on terrorism could be won by intensive military action while failing to recognise the root causes of the problem. More than that, he warned that the use of excessive force could even tend to radicalise Islamic opinion.

These views may be shared by many, but they are far more significant coming from Boyce, who is regarded as a highly professional CDS who is less political than his predecessor, General (now Lord) Guthrie. Guthrie was also held in high regard, not least in Downing Street circles, but was criticised from the right for being too close to Tony Blair. In many ways it was an unfair criticism as Guthrie, whose earlier experience included a period in the SAS, was one of the few top-ranking western military officers who was willing to think long-term and to recognise issues such as the wealth–poverty divide and environmental constraints as future causes of conflict.

In some ways, the views expressed by Boyce last week would be those expected of his predecessor, which is what makes them so interesting. Here is a well-respected professional CDS saying, in very clear language, that 'the war on terror' will not be won unless the circumstances in which al-Qaida and other groups can draw so much support can be understood and changed. That he would express these views in public is a surprise; that he should do so just as the US was intensifying its bombing in south-east Afghanistan is something that any British politician should ponder.

The war in wider context

As the war in Afghanistan is concentrated in a smaller area, it may be developments in the Israeli-Palestinian conflict that have wider implications. After the atrocities in Jerusalem and Haifa at the beginning of the month, the Sharon government responded with considerable force, with Washington effectively agreeing to the action. The response, inevitably, was further action by Palestinian militia, with an even stronger counter-reaction from the Israelis.

The occupied territories of Gaza and the West Bank are now effectively parcelled up into numerous smaller areas under strict Israeli military control. Per capita GNP for the Palestinians has plummeted in recent years and is now about one-tenth of that of the Israelis; there is mass unemployment and even reports of malnutrition. Arafat's position is increasingly weakened, both by the Israelis and by the further radicalisation of Palestinian opinion in the face of what, from their perception, is seen as continued Israeli repression backed by the United States.

In many respects, the occupied territories have been turned into huge open prisons for close to 2 million people, with little scope for movement even between towns and cities within the territories. Even so, most Israelis still feel deeply insecure and are ready to accept the Sharon government's characterisation of Arafat as the promoter of terrorism.

In such a context, the killing of ten Jewish settlers last week in the ambush of a bus on the West Bank is much more significant than most analysts appreciate. An underpinning of Sharon's approach has been the maintenance and even expansion of the settlements, as part of ensuring long-term control of the West Bank (Judea and Samaria), and this requires security for the settlers. Such security is essential because a large proportion of the settlers are not ideologically committed people, but rather those seeking good-quality, low-cost housing.

The development of the settlements has gone hand in hand with substantial security measures, including numerous new strategic roads often bisecting Palestinian areas enabling settlers to move safely between the settlements and Israeli territory where many of them work. All loss of life is a tragedy, but in the Israeli security context, the killing of a large group of settlers by armed Palestinians is actually worse than suicide bombings in Jerusalem or Haifa, as it presages a vulnerability that strikes at the heart of Sharon's policy for the territories.

It is for this reason, especially, that the Sharon administration has been taking such hard action against Palestinians in general and Arafat's people in particular. It is, in effect, being supported by the United States, but the end result will be a further pronounced radicalisation of young Palestinians and a view, through much of the Arab world, that the United States and Israel are together engaged in an anti-Arab campaign in the guise of a war on terror. Whether or not you accept such a view, that is the perception, and it is increasingly widespread in the region.

Indicators – lasers and space weapons

As the war in Afghanistan continued, two small indicators of short- and long-term trends were reported last week. One concerns US-Israeli military relations. An offshoot of recent intensive efforts to develop directed-energy weapons (such as high-power lasers) was an experimental tactical high-energy laser (THEL) that has been used to shoot down a number of Katyusha unguided artillery rockets in firing trials. This was of considerable interest to the Israeli military, who are now negotiating with the US Army to develop an operational variant as a joint project.

The aim would be to deploy, before the end of the decade, a mobile THEL (MTHEL) that would be far less unwieldy than the current experimental form, and would be able to be transported by C-130 transport aircraft and to be moved around rapidly on the back of military trucks. Most of the $250 million so far spent on the THEL has come from the United States but, according to *Jane's Defence Weekly*, the MTHEL project would involve very close US-Israeli co-operation, with each state bearing half of the estimated $350 million development costs. The MTHEL project indicates both the considerable interest in directed energy weapons and the extent of US-Israeli collaboration in leading-edge technologies.

In another development, almost coincident with President Bush's decision to withdraw from the Anti-Ballistic Missile Treaty, it was reported that the US Air Force is planning to develop what is being called a military space plane. Rather like a smaller militarised version of the space shuttle, it would be reusable and could serve multiple functions. These would include being able to respond rapidly to crises by placing military payloads in space, and could even be used as a weapons platform for delivering munitions at targets on earth from space.

It comes at a time of increased interest in space-based directed energy systems, especially the space-based laser (SBL). While the SBL is being developed primarily to destroy ballistic missiles soon after they have been launched, Pentagon studies have already been undertaken to see whether it could be further developed to attack targets on the ground.

Taken together, these developments are both aspects of a potential militarisation of space, with US Space Command seeing it as essential for the United States to control this 'high frontier'. The Afghanistan War has been fought using persistent high-altitude bombing. By 2020, such wars may be fought, at least in part, directly from space itself.

America's theatre is the world
24 December 2001

By the end of the eleventh week of the war, there was a media perception that the conflict in Afghanistan was effectively over and that issues of international terrorism were of less concern. It was a perception that was ended by the concern over a merchant ship intercepted off the south coast of England, en route to London, and by an apparent attempt to explode a bomb on an American Airlines flight from Paris to Miami.

Whether or not either incident had connections to the al-Qaida group, perhaps the more significant issues related to developments in Afghanistan and the Persian Gulf, where there was evidence that the war was far from over and that the next stages of what has been called Phase Two were beginning to develop.

As has so often been the case with the war in Afghanistan, early news reports have been of dubious validity, and evidence available a week or more after particular events frequently casts a different light. There was a widely held view two weeks ago that the core of the al-Qaida network was isolated in the Tora Bora region and that its destruction was imminent. Moreover, the Taliban as a whole was comprehensively defeated, its leaders were likely to be captured and, with this defeat, Afghanistan would return to peace for the first time in more than two decades. Furthermore, all this had been achieved with a minimum of civilian casualties.

The fate of al-Qaida

There is reasonably accurate evidence of substantial al-Qaida casualties in the Tora Bora region, with possibly as many as 200 people being killed, partly through the intensive area bombing by the US, and partly through the action of anti-Taliban militia, working with US and UK Special Forces. At the same time, though, up to 1,500, or possibly more, have escaped the immediate area, many moving into Pakistan. Osama bin Laden has, at the time of writing, escaped capture, and there remains a persistent fear that much of the key leadership of al-Qaida had left Afghanistan around 11 September, with many others leaving in late October as the intensity of the US military action became apparent.

With much support for al-Qaida and the Taliban in north-west Pakistan, it would therefore be possible for the network to retain much of its structure. In any case, it is worth recalling the early reports, shortly after 11 September, that the network was effectively a loose coalition of groups that was fully internationalised, both drawing support from, and operating in, many countries across the world.

In a sense, the US action against the Taliban and those elements of al-Qaida in Afghanistan was actually the most feasible part of a much wider range of actions. Moreover it served a substantial domestic purpose, being likely to prove popular in a country that, even three months after the event, remained deeply affected by the aftermath of the 11 September attacks.

Effects of the bombing

With the scaling down of the air campaign, it has proved possible to get some indications of its effects. As far as can be established, around 10,000 tons of munitions were used in the first eleven weeks, much of it unguided 'dumb' bombs used in area bombing by B-52 and B-1B strategic bombers operating from the US base on the British-controlled island of Diego Garcia in the Indian Ocean.

Repeated early reports indicated substantial civilian casualties but many were discounted as Taliban propaganda. More careful analysis by one US academic, using a wide range of press reports, suggests that over 3,000 civilians have been killed by the bombing – rather more than died in New York and Washington. Other analysts suggest that Taliban militia casualties may number around 5,000, together with several hundred al-Qaida militia.

Overall, the death toll since 11 September may be around 12,000, with one-quarter of those dying in the original attacks on the World Trade Center and the Pentagon. Furthermore, in Afghanistan itself, there is a degree of stability in Kabul and some of the larger towns, but this has been accompanied by a rapid revival of warlordism and banditry in much of the country. The small UN-backed stabilisation force now being assembled in Kabul may eventually extend its work to a few other centres of population, but it would require many tens of thousands of troops to bring order to the country as a whole. There is no international commitment to such a programme.

In any case, this would be unacceptable to the Pentagon, which is concerned primarily to continue the search for the Taliban and al-Qaida leadership, insofar as it is still in Afghanistan. This determination even extends to having ensured that the international force, ostensibly led by the UK, is under the final command of the Pentagon.

Since the easing of large-scale fighting, it has been possible for aid agencies to move food supplies into some of the larger cities, but it has proved much more difficult to transport them into areas in real need. Given that Afghanistan is essentially a country of towns, villages and small farms, what happens in the cities is not indicative of realities across the country. This potentially false picture is strengthened by the lack of reporting by western journalists, an understandable reaction given that eight journalists have already been killed during this war.

Where are the Taliban?

At the end of twelve weeks, it is possible to account for, at the most, 12,000 members of the Taliban militia, including those in captivity, and perhaps 1–2,000 al-Qaida members, very few of the latter being in captivity. What has been surprising is that very few people, either from the Taliban or al-Qaida, have been taken into custody by the United States, either in the hastily constructed prison near Kandahar or on warships in the Arabia Sea.

Given that the Taliban could call on at least 50,000 armed militia and a fairly dispersed leadership, the question arises – where have they gone? In that connection it is worth recalling, once again, that many of the apparent battles in the war were actually rapid occupations of particular towns and cities by diverse anti-Taliban militia following the effective retreat of Taliban forces. This supports the view that, for the most part, Taliban militia have simply melted back into local communities, with their arms and munitions largely intact.

This leads to the key questions as to whether the Taliban retains any cohesion and whether some units are still present as coherent fighting groups in some more remote areas. If so, and it is at least likely, then efforts may be made next spring to resume control of parts of the Pashtun areas, especially if the new government fails to bring stability to the country.

This is an uncomfortable analysis for those who have assumed the war to be at an end, but it is supported by three factors. One, already stated, is that so little of the Taliban and al-Qaida forces have been destroyed, and a second is that there is accumulating evidence that many have moved into Pakistan. The final factor, mentioned in the 17 December article, is that the one group that is not claiming that the war in Afghanistan is over is the Pentagon itself. More US troops have been moved into the country, two secure bases have now been established in the south, and there is every sign that longer-term operations are planned.

Somalia and Iraq – extending the war?

If substantial elements of the al-Qaida network are now in north-west Pakistan, it is possible that the US will put considerable pressure on the Pakistani government to facilitate military operations in the region. This will not be easy, not least because of enduring support for the Taliban and because of the huge complications occasioned by the current tension between India and Pakistan over Kashmir.

In addition to an extension into Pakistan, there would appear to be a developing US interest in operations in Somalia and Yemen, although the Yemeni government may have sought to pre-empt US action there by recent military action against dissidents. Action in Somalia would almost certainly involve the use of Kenya as a base, raising awkward political issues.

The Kenyan government of Daniel Arap Moi has had a formidable reputation for corruption, losing a number of aid programmes as a result. It is therefore particularly keen to aid the United States, but this would be unpopular internally for two quite different reasons. One is that there remains resentment in Kenya over the bombing of the US embassy in Nairobi, mainly because the US rescue squads were seen to have concentrated on the small number of American casualties whereas Kenya lost 250 of its citizens. The other problem is that intervention in Somalia would add to the flow of refugees from that country leading to further difficulties both in north-east Kenya and in Nairobi itself where many past refugees have settled.

Meanwhile, there is some evidence of a build-up of US forces in the Gulf, indicating preparations for action against Iraq. Any such military intervention is unlikely for many weeks, not least because of the time it takes to move forces into the region, a continuing pre-occupation with Afghanistan, and the need to manufacture large quantities of munitions to replace those used in Afghanistan.

One indication of possible action is the establishment of a US Army Headquarters in Kuwait, the HQ concerned being a key component of the army's commitment to US Central Command, the unified military command that covers the Middle East and South-west Asia, including both Afghanistan and Iraq. There are further reports that elements of five different army divisions are preparing for possible deployment to the Gulf early in the New Year, including units that have recently undergone extensive desert warfare training.

What will be indicative in the coming weeks will be whether there are credible reports of CIA/Special Forces units in the Kurdish areas of northern Iraq, as it is likely that any US action would involve an intensive air assault, some limited ground action and substantial help for internal Iraqi opposition forces, especially in the Kurdish areas. Also of note will be any substantial build-up of aircraft carrier battle groups in the Persian Gulf and the Arabian Sea in January and February, especially if Saudi Arabia prevents the United States using bases in its own country.

Very well – alone

One anticipated effect of the atrocities of 11 September would be that the Bush administration would give up its unilateralist leanings and work more closely on multilateral co-operation. Such hopes seem less and less plausible, not least with the withdrawal from the Anti-Ballistic Missile Treaty and the opposition to the strengthening of the Biological and Toxin Weapons Treaty. Two more indicators have now emerged indicating longer-term attitudes.

On 18 December, the *Albuquerque Journal* reported that proposals have been presented to Congress to research and develop a spe-cialised five-kiloton nuclear warhead designed specifically to burrow deep underground and destroy hardened bunkers containing chemical and biological weapons stores. The current US nuclear 'bunker buster', the B61-11, is a larger and more crude nuclear weapon, and conventional weapons are not powerful enough to destroy deeply buried facilities. The *Journal* has a record of accuracy in nuclear matters, not least because it is, in effect, the local newspaper for an area that includes the Los Alamos National Laboratory where nuclear weapons were first developed in the Manhattan Project in the early 1940s.

Critics point out that producing such a 'usable' bomb would make it more likely that a future conflict could mean a greater risk of breaching the nuclear threshold for the first time since 1945. It might also involve the resumption of nuclear testing as this would be a new type of nuclear warhead, whereas the recently deployed B61-11 uses a standard tactical nuclear warhead or 'physics package' with heavily modified casing and fusing.

The other indicator was the astonishing decision to conduct a large-scale battle exercise of the Trident submarine-launched ballistic missile system on 9 December. This exercise, not reported outside of a few specialist defence journals such as *Aviation Week*, involved 'ripple firing' four missiles in quick succession from the USS *Ohio*.

Test firing of single missiles is a fairly frequent procedure but ripple firing is much rarer, and is about the nearest thing that the US Navy ever gets to war-time simulations. The 9 December exercise was the second in six months, itself quite remarkable, but the real significance lies in the timing – undertaking it virtually in parallel with the decision to withdraw from the ABM Treaty. As one critic has remarked, it was a classic 'in your face' statement to the Chinese – that the US now intends to develop missile defences while maintaining the world's most powerful arsenal of strategic nuclear weapons.

A third phase of war
31 December 2001

At a superficial level, one might expect a degree of satisfaction in the Pentagon at the apparent completion of the war in Afghanistan, with the destruction of the Taliban regime and the dispersal of the al-Qaida network's organisation in that country. Instead, there is an almost palpable sense of frustration at the outcome, a frustration that stems from several factors.

The most obvious is the failure, so far, to capture or kill the leaders of the Taliban regime, including Mullah Omar, and the key figures in al-Qaida, most notably Osama bin Laden, whose recent video appears to confirm reports that he moved directly from Kandahar to Pakistan some weeks ago. Related to this is the growing awareness that the great majority of the Taliban have simply melted away from the major towns and cities, often in collusion with supposedly anti-Taliban militia and local warlords.

Similarly, the number of al-Qaida militia that have been captured is a small fraction of those assumed to have been in Afghanistan four months ago. Hundreds were killed, not least around Tora Bora, but many more have moved into Pakistan, along with some elements of the Taliban leadership. There have even been reports of elements of both groups essentially 'buying' their way into Pakistan, paying off anti-Taliban groups to ensure safe passage.

Civilian penalties

Another American frustration has been the difficulties encountered in pursuing the air war against Taliban elements still on the move, the major one being growing opposition from within the new regime in Kabul, not least because of the killing of civilians. Two recent examples caused particular disquiet. One was the destruction of a convoy on its way to the inauguration of the new administration in Kabul, and the other was the attack on the home of a Taliban commander in eastern Afghanistan.

In the first case, the convoy was assumed to be carrying Taliban leaders but this appears to have been incorrect. In any case, the attack extended over several hours, destroying a neighbouring village and killing many people. In the second case at least 25 villagers were killed, and the Taliban leader was not even present. What made the latter incident more problematic was the response of the Chair of the US Joint Chiefs of Staff, General Richard Myers, who commented: 'We think the majority of folks in there would have been Taliban leadership.' This appears to have been wrong but, even so, implied that the killing of the 'minority' of civilians was not of enduring concern.

Such an attitude tends to produce a perception within the Kabul regime that collateral damage is of little importance to the United States, and that Taliban and al-Qaida elements will continue to be pursued with vigour, whatever the effects on ordinary people. In some ways it is an inevitable consequence of the failure of the war to deliver the leadership of either organisation, a failure compounded by the probable location of many key elements in Pakistan.

Another aspect of the recent bombings that is significant is that it lends credence to the view that civilian casualties were very high during the air war in November and December. At that time, almost all reports of civilian casualties were dismissed as Taliban propaganda. This can no longer be given as an excuse if the new regime is making similar claims. There have also been reports from observers travelling to some of the areas subject to intensive US bombing that the effects were devastating. In short, recent independent estimates of more than 3,000 civilians killed in the bombing look all too plausible.

The position of Pakistan

Although Pakistan has appeared to offer substantial assistance to the United States, Washington has been careful to limit its demands and the Pakistani regime has been lax in the fulfilment of stated commitments. This is hardly surprising, given that the Taliban regime was fully backed by Pakistan and was seen as a way of ensuring a pliant Afghanistan that would not come under the influence of the Northern Alliance with its links to India.

If the United States is to further pursue its campaign against the Taliban and al-Qaida then it has either to take military action in Pakistan, or persuade the Musharraf regime to do so. Both options present problems. While there have been some US military units operating from bases in Pakistan, these have been relatively few in number and have conducted their operations largely in secret. There has, in consequence, been relatively little in the way of anti-American action. This would be likely to change if the US was to take direct military action within Pakistan, even if the Musharraf regime agreed.

US action would probably follow a broadly similar pattern to that of the war in Afghanistan, with Special Forces units working in concert with air attacks. In such circumstances, civilian casualties would be likely, with predictable effects on public opinion and the prospect of real opposition to the Musharraf regime.

The second option would be for the Pakistani authorities to take firm action themselves, but this is made highly unlikely given the current dangerous confrontation with India. While the Pakistani authorities may have been aware of the recent paramilitary attack on the Indian parliament, and are certainly aware of the actions of para-militaries in Kashmir, there is a reluctance to take steps to control them, not least because Pakistan believes that the war in Afghanistan has created far more problems for it than it has solved.

Pakistan now finds itself with an unfriendly regime to the west, and a US attitude that is increasingly pro-India and determined to continue the containment and destruction of the Taliban and al-Qaida. At the same time, there is a real fear in Islamabad of the current Indian build-up, not least because India is far stronger in terms of conven-tional military forces, and is led by a notably nationalist government which is particularly aggrieved at the attack on the parliament – widely seen in India as a Pakistani-backed attempt to assassinate key elements of the political leadership.

One strong possibility is that Washington will use the current Indo-Pakistan crisis to put pressure on the Islamabad government, essentially offering to use its considerable influence in New Delhi in return for stronger Pakistani action against the Taliban and al-Qaida. It is, though, a dangerous strategy, not least because one of the immediate effects of the Indian military build-up is to encourage Pakistan to withdraw military forces from the Afghan border. Fur-thermore, any confrontation between India and Pakistan is inherently dangerous, not least because both states now have nuclear weapons. The prospect for untoward crisis escalation is present, and it would make far more sense for Washington to take direct steps to do what it can to defuse the crisis rather than seek to manipulate it as a means of putting pressure on Islamabad.

The wider picture

In all of this it still makes sense for us to remind ourselves of a few salient points in relation to al-Qaida. The organisation seems to have been part of a loose amalgam of groups, mainly centred on the Middle East and concerned, in their different ways, with Israeli control of

Jerusalem and the occupied territories, the US military presence in the Gulf and the existence of illegitimate regimes in the western Gulf states, especially Saudi Arabia.

Different paramilitary groups have targeted different aspects of these forces, with al-Qaida mainly concerned with the United States and the Saudi regime. While using Afghanistan as a significant centre, especially for training, it has had monetary support from many rich individuals, mainly in western Gulf states, and has a network of operatives and associates in many countries. Osama bin Laden may be a significant leader, but has taken on, or been assigned, a figurehead role that may well have made him appear far more significant than he actually is.

The US intervention in the Afghan civil war and the fall of the Taliban regime has no doubt done damage to the al-Qaida network, but much of the network appears to have dispersed, and it is by no means certain that the damage is irreparable. It remains likely that much of the US reaction to the atrocities of 11 September was foreseen.

US political figures speak of the reaction of the past few months as being Phase One of a longer 'war on terrorism'. It should be assumed that, to the perpetrators, the attacks of 11 September may have been Phase Two or Three in their own war against the United States and its allies in the Gulf (e.g. the 1993 World Trade Center attack, the 1998 US embassy bombings, and operations in Saudi Arabia and Yemen). On that basis, the recent reversals in Afghanistan may shortly prompt the instigation of another phase, directed against the United States or its allies in the Gulf or elsewhere.

3

A New American Century?

By the end of 2001, it looked as though the war in Afghanistan was over. Senior politicians in Washington were happy to talk of victory, but military opinion was much more cautious, not least because fighting continued in parts of the country and there had been an almost complete inability to kill or capture the Taliban or al-Qaida leadership. Furthermore, intelligence agencies were by no means convinced that the capability of al-Qaida and its associates to stage paramilitary attacks had diminished.

Even so, these problems did nothing to diminish the consolidation of a vigorous international security paradigm in Washington, in which the longer-term vision of a 'New American Century' provided the context for a notable State of the Union Address in January 2002. President Bush's speech, and other administration pronouncements, made it clear that there was an axis of evil of rogue states that stretched well beyond Afghanistan and its support for al-Qaida. Iraq, Iran and North Korea were "first-division" members of the axis, followed by Libya, Syria and Cuba.

In support of the widening war, defence budgets were intended to increase substantially and the US military would develop new military bases across Central Asia while increasing their aid to counter-insurgency forces in Colombia, the Philippines and elsewhere.

This was part of a wider view in Washington of the need to develop the 'benign imperium', a stable world comprising a liberal polity in an essentially free market, modelled on the US system. It was an outlook that was radically different from that of many opinion formers and much public opinion in the 'majority world' away from the countries of the Atlantic community, and would also lead to further fractures in the Euro-American relationship.

Oil and the 'war on terrorism':
why is the United States in the Gulf?
9 January 2002

As the US bombing campaign in Afghanistan resumes, it is important to assess the core strategic reason for American persistence – its perceived need to retain its military presence in Saudi Arabia.

First, in the Afghan campaign itself, the civilian death toll is rising, and US Marines and Special Forces are seeking out elements of the Taliban leadership. After three months of war, one of the main aims – to kill or capture the leadership elements of both the al-Qaida network and the Taliban regime – had achieved few results, one reason for the distinct lack of triumphalism in the Pentagon.

According to a press briefing from the US embassy in Islamabad, given on 26 December, 34 out of 42 members of the al-Qaida command structure remained at large, with six believed dead and two captured. Of the 27 members of the Taliban leadership, one had been killed, two had been captured and 24 remained at large. There have been a handful of further instances of the capture or killing of senior Taliban and al-Qaida figures since 26 December, but it would be wise to expect that US military operations will continue through the winter, with very heavy pressure put on the Musharraf regime in Pakistan to seek out those elements of both organisations now in north-west Pakistan.

As operations continue, it is becoming apparent that there is a central tension between US attempts to carry out their military operations and the need of the regime in Kabul to bring stability to the country. It also explains the continued US opposition to any large-scale peacekeeping operation, the stabilisation force so far agreed being a small number of units operating in Kabul and a few other locations.

In these circumstances, and with the conflict set to continue, it is appropriate to reflect on the wider context in which al-Qaida and other paramilitary organisations have developed in the region. Given that US operations may, in due course, extend to attempting to destroy Saddam Hussein's regime in Iraq, it is worth looking, in particular, at the nature and evolution of the US military presence in the region.

The roots of paramilitary action

Paramilitary coalitions and networks in the Middle East and South-west Asia operate, in part, from religious convictions, not least in relation to what they see as the bias of the United States towards Israel and the latter's control of Jerusalem. Some of them also develop from a persistent resistance to the presence of US military forces in the Persian Gulf region, and especially in Saudi Arabia. This is particularly true of the al-Qaida network, the 11 September attacks forming part of a strategy that has developed over more than a decade and is unlikely to be ended by the short-term, if substantial, disruptions caused by the current war.

The Saudi connection is central, especially if one takes into account that the United States and its Israeli ally are together 'occupying' the three holiest places in Islam. A common feature of the long-term paramilitary strategy is to force the United States from the region, to defeat Israel and to ensure the downfall of those neo-feudal elite regimes that are considered to have 'sold out' to the United States.

The US presence in the Gulf is not recent, there are established historical and geopolitical reasons for it and there is little likelihood of any withdrawal. Analysing this is an important component of understanding the motives of those bitterly opposed to the US presence in the region as a whole.

The first oil shock

The development of the oil reserves of the Persian Gulf was originally undertaken primarily by oil companies with European connections, but US oil companies became highly significant in Iran and Saudi Arabia, and there was a close relationship between the US and Iran in particular from the 1950s. Until around 1970, the very extensive oilfields of Texas, Louisiana, California and elsewhere enabled the United States to be self-sufficient for oil, but rising demand and slowly depleting reserves meant a dependency on cheap imported oil began to develop in the early 1970s.

Meanwhile, the oil-producing countries began to organise themselves, with the Organisation of Petroleum Exporting Countries (OPEC) being formed in 1960. For more than a decade it remained a very weak producer group, but by 1973 it had developed a degree of unity and strength of purpose that was to lead to the 'oil shock' of 1973–74.

The prompt for this came in October 1973, when Arab members of OPEC attempted to use the oil weapon to curtail Israeli military gains during the latter part of the Yom Kippur/Ramadan War, and these resulted in a series of events that included severe oil shortages together with price rises of about 450 per cent over eight months. OPEC's action caused profound shock in the United States and Western Europe and demonstrated a vulnerability that had previously been discounted.

As a result, during and after this crisis, assessments were made in Washington of the likely success of US military intervention in the Gulf should oil supplies be substantially interrupted. These assessments indicated that the US simply did not have the military means to intervene with any prospect of success, especially as it lacked the capacity for rapid deployment of appropriate forces.

What made this more worrying was that the American dependency on imported oil was steadily increasing, and most of the best new reserves were being found in and around the Persian Gulf. Even the massive oilfield at Prudhoe Bay in northern Alaska, developed in the early 1970s, represented barely 1 per cent of known world oil reserves at the time.

During the latter part of the 1970s, intensive military planning was therefore undertaken and this resulted in the establishment of the multiservice Joint Rapid Deployment Task Force, known more commonly as the Rapid Deployment Force, in 1980. Although theoretically capable of deployment anywhere in the world, the emphasis from the start was on the Persian Gulf region.

Reagan and CENTCOM

Although the Rapid Deployment Force originated after the oil shortages instigated by OPEC, the Reagan administration developed it into the much larger Central Command (CENTCOM) to counter possible Soviet aggression in the Gulf. This was during the heightened Cold War tensions of the early 1980s, with CENTCOM established as a full regional military command covering an arc of 19 countries stretching from Kenya to Pakistan across the Middle East.

CENTCOM could call on over 300,000 military personnel including the Third Army, the Ninth Air Force, three carrier battle groups, elements of Strategic Air Command and substantial intelligence, reconnaissance and Special Forces units. During the 1980s, substantial air bases and other facilities were constructed in the western Gulf states, especially in Saudi Arabia, far larger than local forces required, so that CENTCOM forces could be moved in if required. The British island territory of Diego Garcia in the Indian Ocean was built up into a very large logistical centre, the Ilois inhabitants having been previously 'resettled' against their will in Mauritius.

Although intended to operate in the face of a threat from the Soviet Union, the Iraqi invasion of Kuwait in 1990 provided CENTCOM with the opportunity to form the core of the coalition that ousted Iraq from Kuwait six months later. In the process, all of the pre-positioning and base construction activities of the 1980s came into their own.

After the Gulf War, the United States maintained a military presence in many western Gulf states including the establishment of the Fifth Fleet in the Gulf and, for the first time, a permanent presence of significant forces in Saudi Arabia. Thus, just as US help had enabled opposition forces to evict the Soviet Union from Afghanistan, so the US was there to be seen as an occupying force in the greatly more significant Islamic Kingdom of Saudi Arabia.

Oil and US security

While the continued presence of large US forces in the Gulf can be explained in part by the ongoing confrontation with Iraq, this in turn is only understandable in terms of the geopolitics of oil. This stems from two features – the remarkable quantity of reserves in the Gulf region, and the steadily increasing dependence of the United States on imported oil.

The decade of the 1990s shows this particularly clearly. Take oil reserves first: in 1990, the United States oil reserves represented 3.4 per cent of world oil reserves, whereas Kuwait alone had 9.5 per cent and the Gulf states had 63.5 per cent. Ten years later US reserves had declined to 2.8 per cent of the world total whereas the Gulf states now had 66.5 per cent. Then look at oil dependency – in 1990, the US imported 42 per cent of its total oil requirements; ten years later this had risen to 60 per cent.

Moreover, the rate of discovery of new reserves in the United States was not keeping pace with demand, whereas discovery of reserves in the Gulf region was exceeding production. Iraq, for example, increased its proved oil reserves in the decade up to 2000 by a figure rather more than half of that of *total* US reserves in 2000.

The Bush administration is pinning much of its hope on intensive oil exploration in the Arctic National Wildlife Refuge, east of the Prudhoe Bay oilfield in northern Alaska. But there are serious doubts as to whether there really are large reserves there, the most recent estimate from the US Geological Survey giving a best case estimate of 11.8 billion barrels, about the same as the original Prudhoe Bay field. In other words, Alaska is not the answer (see *New Scientist*, 5 January 2001, for an informative article on this).

Oil dependency, and the US determination to ensure security of supplies, is therefore at the heart of the US presence in the Gulf. Because of trends in production, consumption and discovery of reserves, this policy is highly unlikely to change. In much of the Arab world, and elsewhere in South-west Asia, it is seen as a form of neo-colonial occupation, in which a distant superpower retains control of a key resource in its own interests. From this perspective, both the Kingdom of the Two Holy Places, and Jerusalem, are under the heel of US military forces or (in the latter case) their Israeli proxy.

Although there are important subsidiary factors, this is a major reason for a deep and abiding antipathy to the United States among a significant proportion of the region's population, from which radical paramilitary coalitions have developed. In recent years these have attempted extensive paramilitary actions against the United States. Some have been intercepted. Others, like the 1993 World Trade Center bombing, did not achieve their full aims. Still others did succeed, including the bombing of the Khobar Towers barracks complex in Dhahran in 1996, the US embassy bombings in Nairobi and Dar es Salaam and the attack on the USS *Cole* in Aden harbour.

Only with the attacks of 11 September 2001 did the full impact of these developments come to the fore, but hardly any connection has so far been made between the paramilitary coalitions responsible and some of the core underlying motivations relating to energy geopolitics. The much-vaunted 'war on terrorism' is aimed at destroying these paramilitary coalitions without apparently facing up to these motivations. The destruction of the paramilitaries may well not be possible. Even if it is, it will have little more than a short-term effect unless some of the key underlying factors empowering their development are recognised.

A change of policy?

The US military presence in the most significant country, Saudi Arabia, is actually quite small – fewer than 10,000 people, so the obvious question is why is this considered so important? Would it not make sense to withdraw from Saudi Arabia, thus removing a substantial part of the motivation for al-Qaida and other groups? There are several reasons why this is unlikely in the extreme.

One is that any withdrawal would be regarded in Washington as a defeat for US Gulf policy and would be considered a victory for anti-US sentiments in the region. In addition, if the US withdrew from Saudi Arabia, regional anti-US groups would focus intensively on US forces in neighbouring countries, especially Kuwait, Bahrain and even Oman.

There are also substantial military reasons for the presence in Saudi Arabia. One is that the bases are located at some distance from the perceived major threat of Iraq, whereas Kuwait is, so to speak, on the front line. Secondly, the huge port facilities that were used to pour troops and equipment into the region in 1990–91 are in Saudi Arabia, and provide a bridgehead for reinforcements. Finally, if the US were to withdraw from the region, it would be almost impossible to return in a time of crisis – it is hugely easier to reinforce existing forces than to move in from scratch.

There is another motivation for maintaining forces in Saudi Arabia – the security of the House of Saud. This is very much a double-edged sword in that keeping forces in Saudi Arabia means they are available to help respond to internal instability, but their very presence can foster that instability. In the final analysis, though, Saudi Arabia has more than a quarter of the world's entire oil reserves, nearly ten times as much as the United States. That alone means that any possibility of withdrawal is highly unlikely.

For the present, the United States shows no sign whatsoever of attempting to control its addiction to oil. Indeed, with the Bush administration in power, any talk of doing so is treated with near contempt. As a consequence, the Persian Gulf will be seen as of the utmost importance to US security, and almost any means will be used to ensure its stability. For this reason, if for no other, paramilitary groups will evolve and respond, and the 'war on terrorism' will continue for many years to come.

US entrenchment across Central Asia
14 January 2002

Coverage of the conflict in Afghanistan is now limited to relatively brief reports in the inside pages of more substantial newspapers, though the specialist defence press remains full of it. US military operations have continued at a surprisingly high level of intensity, with marines and Special Forces encountering resistance in several parts of the country, and air bombardments being, at times, almost as heavy as in November.

While the interim government has established a presence of sorts in Kabul, the predicted problems of lawlessness, warlordism and banditry have developed apace. Without very considerable outside aid – far greater than is planned for the international stabilisation force – there seems little prospect of order being established in much of the country in the coming months.

At the same time, if a view is taken of the region as a whole, it becomes clear that the United States has succeeded in establishing a military presence without precedent. This gives it a remarkably powerful position in the area that could, in turn, lead to an eventual counter-reaction.

The United States in the region

As was mentioned in an earlier piece (10 December 2001), one extension of American activity was the establishment of a US military presence at Burgas Air Force Base in eastern Bulgaria, the first time foreign troops had been based in that country since Soviet troops left in 1946. Burgas is used to support aerial refuelling, and this is likely to continue as its geographical position is very useful in terms of planes in transit to new bases in Central Asia.

There has also been a build-up in the Persian Gulf, with army units deployed to Kuwait and the further build-up of the Al-Udeid

Air Base in Qatar. This latter base, construction of which only started in 2000, has a 15,000-foot runway, one of the longest in the region and, according to the *Los Angeles Times*, is costing around a billion dollars to complete.

These developments in the Gulf are in addition to the substantial US presence in the region for the ten years prior to 11 September. This includes major bases and pre-positioned supplies in Saudi Arabia, Kuwait and Bahrain and the huge logistics supply centre and air base on Diego Garcia in the Indian Ocean.

Even so, what is much more significant is the expanding US presence in Central and South Asia. The build-up in Pakistan has been done with as little publicity as possible, but it is known that the US armed forces are using several bases, including one at Shamsi, the site of last Wednesday's crash of a Marine Corps KC-130 tanker as it was approaching the airfield. The plane had been on what was termed a multistop mission, originating at another base at Jacobabad, also in Pakistan.

Another indication of a long-term deployment is the decision to maintain two carrier battle groups together with amphibious warfare ships with several thousand Marines on board in the northern Arabian Sea. The current deployment runs through to the end of March but is expected to be extended repeatedly. This is in addition to other warships serving with the Fifth Fleet in the Persian Gulf.

In Afghanistan itself, the Marines who established control of Kandahar Airport are being replaced by 1,000 troops of the 101st Airborne Division. This number could be doubled and indicates a long-term presence – Marines tend to establish facilities and then move on, whereas the army tends to bed down for a longer time. Elsewhere in Afghanistan, a substantial US presence has been established, again with minimum publicity, at the old Soviet air base at Bagram north of Kabul, scene of a small UK deployment back in November.

The move into Central Asia

Perhaps most interesting of all is the manner in which an extensive and substantial US presence is being established in three countries of Central Asia. Over 1,000 soldiers of the 10th Mountain Division are now firmly established at Khanabad Air Base in Uzbekistan, with substantial repair and renovation work under way. The Uzbekistan government has a highly questionable human rights record but this does not seem to be an issue.

In neighbouring Tajikistan, three possible sites for new US bases have been examined, at Kulyab, Khojand and Turgan-Tiube. And in Kyrgyzstan, a new base is already under construction at Bishkek. According to the *New York Times* this will be a substantial facility with up to 3,000 troops and will serve as a transportation hub for the region.

What this all amounts to is a reversal of the situation at the end of the Cold War, when US forces withdrew from many of their bases encircling the Soviet Union. Now that the oil-bearing regions of the Persian Gulf and the Caspian Basin have become so significant, and with anti-US movements rife in the region, a substantial military presence is deemed necessary to maintain control. In overall terms, perhaps as many as 60,000 US military personnel are now based in the region at up to 20 bases and on large numbers of warships at sea.

The implications of this for Russia, China and Islamic opinion could be hugely significant in the coming months and years; and it may yet be that the interests of al-Qaida and other paramilitary networks, in seeking an enhanced anti-American attitude, will be realised in due course. Certainly, one effect of the 11 September attacks has been to change the military geography of a substantial part of South-west and Central Asia.

Elsewhere ...

Away from Afghanistan, the Maoist insurgency in Nepal has become so serious that the government is asking the United States to provide military equipment. Although not widely supported outside of South Asia, the six-year insurgency has already cost 2,000 lives and the rebels are reported to control some 40 per cent of the country. They number around 7–12,000 but have succeeded in maintaining their position against government forces of 45,000. A US military mission visited Kathmandu last month and it is probable that the US will extend its traditional support for military training to include a range of counter-insurgency equipment.

Meanwhile, in Washington, it has become clear that President Bush's much-vaunted announcement that he will cut US strategic nuclear arsenals substantially over the next few years is not quite so straightforward as, at first, it looked. It now appears that a substantial proportion of the withdrawn warheads will be put into store and will be capable of being redeployed later if considered necessary.

There are also indications that the Department of Energy may consider a new round of nuclear weapons tests. This would cripple any chance of the Comprehensive Test Ban Treaty surviving, at least in the short term, and would make it much easier for countries such as China and possibly Russia to resume testing. While the reported rationale is to ensure that nuclear weapons stocks are reliable, there are indications that new nuclear warhead designs are now being considered – specifically, a new class of earth-penetrating warheads for destroying deeply buried targets such as underground bunkers or cave complexes.

Right back at the start of the war, soon after the attacks of 11 September, some analysts argued that one of the aims of the perpetrators was to incite a strong US military response, preferably with a much greater US presence in the region, in the belief that this would result in an eventual violent anti-American reaction.

If this was the case, then they have certainly succeeded in the first aspect. Muslim support for bin Laden's archaic extremism may be much less than he would have wished. A ferocious US response has so far been sufficiently targeted not to have stimulated significant popular or Islamic regime opposition. But if the geostrategic investment of Central Asia, with a network of bases, also combines with a determined attempt to ignore all treaties that might hinder the further development of America's technological lead, then over the coming decades this could incite Islamic and non-Islamic states alike into an anti-Washington alliance that could include both Russia and China.

United States unilateralism – still going strong?
22 January 2002

In the immediate aftermath of 11 September, there was a widespread belief that the US would realise that multilateral co-operation would be the only way to respond to the atrocities. Moreover, it was believed that this would be part of a wider appreciation in Washington that the unilateralist attitude that had been such a prominent part of the

Bush administration's approach to international relations would come to an end. Four months after the attacks and more than three months into the 'war on terrorism', how does it look? Have we entered a new era of co-operation, has nothing changed, or has the culture of the Bush administration even been strengthened by recent events?

George Bush's first six months

The 2000 presidential election was so closely run, with Bush's victory ultimately dependent on a handful of votes and 'chads', that many commentators expected the new administration to seek a political consensus in its early policy developments. Not a bit of it. Across the political landscape, and especially in foreign relations, a conservative agenda was rapidly implemented.

A critical approach was taken to UN negotiations on the control of light weapons, there was a much more cautious stance on the strengthening of the biological weapons convention; there was opposition to proposals for talks to prevent the weaponisation of space; and there were clear indications that the US might withdraw from the 1972 Anti-Ballistic Missile (ABM) Treaty while proceeding with plans for a national missile defence system, whatever the effect this might have in Moscow and Beijing. On regional policy, the US ceased negotiations with North Korea and was decidedly disinterested in the Middle East peace agenda.

Perhaps most significant, at least in the view of some European governments, was the decision to withdraw from the Kyoto Protocols on climate change. By the middle of last year, it was abundantly clear that talk of consensus was eyewash and the Bush administration was firmly in the grip of a unilateralist international agenda. Even while this was evolving, EU states were taking a different view, with a high-level EU delegation of North Korea, a renewed commitment to the Middle East and a determination to proceed with the Kyoto process, even without the United States.

There are, though, two caveats to this 'raw' view of US foreign relations. One is that many of these attitudes were there well before the 2000 election. In the latter years of the Clinton administration, and with Congress in Republican hands, there had been other examples of a unilateralist approach, including opposition to the proposed International Criminal Court, criticisms of negotiations on a land mine ban, and a Senate refusal to ratify the Comprehensive Test Ban Treaty (CTBT).

The other caveat is that US policy behaviour since Bush came to power has always been a mix of the multilateral and unilateral. This was put memorably by the right-wing commentator, Charles Krauthammer, writing in the Washington-based *Weekly Standard* of 4 June last year:

> Multipolarity, yes, when there is no alternative. But not when there is. Not when we have the unique imbalance of power that we enjoy today – and that has given the international community a stability and essential tranquility it had not known for at least a century.
>
> The international environment is far more likely to enjoy peace under a single hegemon. Moreover, we are not just any hegemon. We run a uniquely benign imperium.

This view lies at the heart of Republican thinking on international affairs and contrasts markedly with the view from Europe, but it is, in turn, part of a wider world-view where there is some resonance with European political opinion.

The benign imperium

The conviction that America's is a benign imperium stems from a belief that there is only one economic system appropriate for the world community and that this is framed in a particular political context. The system is the globalised free market and the context is liberal democracy. The belief in the free market is fundamental and was massively strengthened by the collapse of the Soviet system.

The Republican Right's interpretation of this view goes further. It holds that the United States has an historic mission to be a civilising force in world affairs, shaping economic and political relationships through business, governmental and other processes to ensure a world economy and polity that is in the American image. It is, necessarily, a global context that is persistently beneficial to the United States, but this does not diminish the sense of mission.

The manner in which the world-view has come to the fore in the past few years has an interesting resonance with the late 1970s. Then,

Jimmy Carter was embattled with Republican forces advocating a vigorous rearming of America to defeat the Soviet threat. In the run-up to the 1980 election, groups such as High Frontier and the Committee on the Present Danger sought assiduously to portray the Carter administration as soft on the Soviets, in contrast to the noble aims of the Republican challenger, Ronald Reagan. Many of those associated with this thinking went on to be influential members of the Reagan administration.

In a similar manner, groups active in the late 1990s focused on the crucial need for US leadership of the globalised world. Most notable was the Project for the New American Century, set up in 1997, with its statement of principles asking, 'Does the United States have the resolve to shape a new century favourable to American principles and interests?' In answering its own question, the Project went on to argue that it is necessary 'to accept responsibility for America's unique role in preserving and extending an international order friendly to our security, our prosperity and our principles'. Among its supporters are Donald Rumsfeld, Secretary of Defense, and Vice-President Dick Cheney.

Such thinking underlies much of the current US approach to international affairs but, in one subtle way, it goes further than this, with a refusal to entertain the idea that there can be any legitimate alternative. This is simply unthinkable, not least because to accept the possibility of alternatives implies that the dominant model may not be fully valid. In this world-view there is an assumption that any other approach or analysis must be either deeply wrong-headed or, if not, malign. As with the war on terrorism, so more generally, 'if you are not with us you are against us'.

The triple dynamic of go-it-alone

Has this mind-set, illustrated by so many actions in the early part of last year, been altered by the attacks on the World Trade Center and the Pentagon? Away from the war in Afghanistan, the indications are of no change. The US government confirmed its opposition to the strengthening of the biological weapons convention in early December and the nuclear warhead cuts that had been announced a month earlier turned out to be plans to put the weapons into storage, not dismantle them. The Anti-Ballistic Missile Treaty was formally abandoned and, the same week, the US Navy staged a rare multiple test-firing of its Trident nuclear missile.

In relation to the war itself, there have been frequent instances of the US minimising other involvements, even to the point of discouraging the UK from contributing regular armed forces to Afghanistan for several key weeks of the war. Meanwhile, numerous prisoners have been shipped to Cuba where they are neither prisoners of war nor criminals, yet face the prospect of trial by military tribunals meeting in secret and without prospect of appeal. US troops have now commenced co-operative counter-insurgency training in the Philippines and there are reported to be Special Forces operating in Somalia. Perhaps most significant has been the rapid and unexpected development and consolidation of a whole string of military bases in Central Asia, including Afghanistan, Uzbekistan, Tajikistan and Pakistan.

On this evidence, there seems little doubt that 'unilateralism rules OK', and three factors help to explain this. The first is that the World Trade Center and Pentagon attacks were particularly traumatic for the Republican Right. Attacking the centre of US commercial power, and closing down the New York Stock Exchange for several days, as well as damaging the Pentagon, struck at the heart of the belief in the new American century and required a vigorous and sustained military response. For a brief moment, the US had lost control and it was imperative that it be regained immediately.

Secondly, the war in Afghanistan appears, on the surface, to have gone well. That, at least, is the opinion of conservative commentators, even if it is not shared by the military leadership which is much more cautious. An apparent victory in Afghanistan is proof of US power and an encouragement to use it whenever and wherever necessary.

Finally, there should have been no reason to expect the Bush administration to have behaved any differently. The belief in the mission of the United States to run the world – to bestow the benign imperium – is deep-rooted in the new generation of Republican thinkers, and it has, if anything, been strengthened by the events of the past four months. American power is now dominant and its limitations are minimal. Before long there may be more terrible examples of the limits to power and the innate vulnerabilities of an urban-industrial superpower, but, for now, the new American century is becoming firmly entrenched, whatever the rest of the world might think.

The logistics of complexity
29 January 2002

Within Afghanistan the war continues, with further bombing and a wide range of actions by US Special Forces. Several thousand US troops are now in Afghanistan itself, together with 1,500 in neighbouring Pakistan and Uzbekistan and some 3,000 due to establish the new base in Kyrgyzstan.

Although there is now little press reporting of the ongoing war, it would appear that a number of al-Qaida units are still active in Afghanistan, even though most have long since gone through to Pakistan. What is surprising is that there is still military action involving Taliban militia, whereas the expectation had been that they would have melted back into their own villages and towns, at least until the spring.

In early January, US bombers made repeated raids on an underground complex in eastern Afghanistan near the village of Zawar, and Marines from the base at Kandahar discovered a much smaller underground network close to the base itself.

On 24 January, Special Forces attacked two al-Qaida compounds about 60 miles north of Kandahar. Initially they were reported to have killed more than a dozen people while capturing al-Qaida and Taliban militia, but later reports indicated that they had mistakenly attacked a compound containing anti-Taliban leaders who had actually been negotiating a surrender with local Taliban militia. In the attack, villagers of Hazar Qadam insisted that 15 pro-government local leaders had been killed.

Refugees, lawlessness and unexploded bombs

Earlier predictions of lawlessness and refugee movements as a consequence of the war are, sadly, being proved right. In mid-January there were reports of at least 50,000 people camped either side of the Afghanistan–Pakistan border, most of them in desperate conditions.

They form part of a much larger number of displaced people, thought to number 700,000 in the southern part of Afghanistan, with many of them fleeing robbery, banditry and the near-collapse of any semblance of law and order.

Added to this is the problem of unexploded ordnance, particularly the 'bomblets' from cluster munitions that have been widely used by US strike aircraft. While efforts are being made by UN de-mining groups to find and defuse these bomblets, their location is often unclear and they are even light enough to be carried into streams and rivers by heavy winter rain.

In the Herat area alone, 41 people have been killed and a similar number injured since the cluster bombs were dropped in November. A further problem is that the presence of unexploded bomblets in any rural area serves as a considerable discouragement to farmers to work the land, especially when it comes to ploughing and sowing seeds for the new growing season.

The international presence

Fairly substantial international aid is now promised to the Karzai administration in Kabul, although it falls far short of what most independent analysts believe is required to restore Afghanistan to some degree of normality. In Kabul itself, the International Security Assistance Force (ISAF) is beginning to establish itself, with its prime functions being to aid security in Kabul, develop future security structures and assist with reconstruction.

ISAF will, though, operate only in Kabul itself, and will have little or no effect on the much wider problems of disorder and lawlessness that are plaguing much of the country. The UN deputy special envoy to Afghanistan, Francesc Vendrell, is reported as saying that about 30,000 peacekeeping troops would be needed to maintain order in the country as a whole, far more than the small ISAF group committed to the Kabul area.

This force of 5,000 troops is to be drawn from an extraordinary range of countries, with Britain providing the lead with 1,800 troops, including the headquarters, followed by Germany (800), France (550), and Italy and Spain (300 each). The Netherlands and Greece follow with about 100 each, followed by smaller numbers from Austria, Belgium, Bulgaria, Denmark, Finland, New Zealand, Norway, Portugal, Romania and Sweden. The only Islamic state to provide troops is Turkey (260), although states such as Jordan are providing humanitarian assistance.

Quite separate from ISAF are the combat forces now working alongside the US. Britain had Special Forces involved in Afghanistan almost from the start, but Australia, Canada, France, Norway and New Zealand have also had small contingents involved. More surprisingly, Canada has now committed a 750-strong combat group to work with elements of the US 101st Airborne Division based at Kandahar.

So it is almost entirely western states that are operating in Afghanistan. The absence of troops from Islamic states will strengthen the impression that there is a religious divide in Bush's 'war on terrorism'. Within this situation, there are some unexpected political aspects, the most significant being the role of the French.

The French move in

Many commentators have remarked on the manner in which the United States has developed its military presence in the region since 11 September, with a chain of bases across South-west and Central Asia. Almost as significant, but largely missed, is the rapid increase in the French military presence in many different guises.

Their contingent in the ISAF currently numbers about 200 out of the planned total of 550; but a Commando force of around 50 Marines is also based in the Kabul area, apparently not part of ISAF. Over in Mazar-e-Sharif, the French have 240 troops engaged in airport reconstruction and offering protection to a field hospital established by a Jordanian medical unit.

French forces are supported by a transport unit of C-130 and C-160 aircraft based in Dushanbe in Tajikistan, and the French government has reached an agreement with Kyrgyzstan to base strike aircraft and tankers at a base there. It is seeking agreement for a similar basing arrangement in Uzbekistan. France has also been involved in maritime reconnaissance flights using land-based aircraft. The logistics operation for its Asian regional commitments is the Villacoublay Air Force Base near Paris.

Meanwhile, a large French naval force is operating in the Arabian Sea, providing most of the 4,200-strong force supporting US operations. Centred on the new nuclear-powered aircraft carrier, *Charles de Gaulle*, and supported by three frigates, a nuclear-powered submarine, minesweepers and support ships, the task force's aircraft had, by mid-January, completed 200 aircraft sorties and had stopped and searched over 400 ships.

The *Charles de Gaulle* normally carries a force of 16 Super Etandard strike aircraft but has recently embarked several of the new Rafale fighters that are likely to be used operationally for the first time over Afghanistan.

The official French line is that all of the forces are there in support of the United States. Independent observers see it rather differently, as more of a traditional French approach: making abundantly sure that France has a sufficient piece of the action, as Central Asia is opened up to stronger western influence.

A strong French presence has at least two political advantages – it positions France in a region with considerable resource potential, and it gives a firm impression of a commitment to the US war on terrorism while helping to ensure that the United States is not the only state to increase its influence in the region.

Saudi-American tensions

The recent press reports of strong differences of opinion between Saudi Arabia and the United States are not unexpected, but they represent a serious problem for Washington, given that Saudi Arabia is such a key location for US forces in the Gulf. There are two separate issues at work, and together they complicate the situation.

The first element is that some sections of the Saudi government rightly regard the US presence as one of the main motivations driving the development of organisations such as al-Qaida. If the US was to leave Saudi Arabia, these sections believe that would greatly relieve the pressures on the regime. They point out that the main growth of the anti-government groups has taken place since the US came into Saudi Arabia in 1990.

The other element is that some senior US armed forces officers would prefer the US to leave Saudi Arabia because of restrictions already placed on their activities by the Saudi authorities. A notable example of this took place back in December 1998 when the US launched the major Desert Fox military operation against Iraq.

On that occasion, the Saudis refused to let the US use its strike aircraft operating from the Prince Sultan Air Force Base for attacks on Iraq, and refused even to let the US deploy the aircraft to other bases in the region. This severely limited the extent of the operation, not least because the planes at Prince Sultan AFB included the F-15E Strike Eagle bombers, intended to form the core of the operation.

This sent a powerful message to planners in the Pentagon that the US simply did not have free rein for its forces in the Kingdom, and raised questions over future operations.

Even so, the bottom line among the political powers in Washington is that Saudi Arabia is of such immense importance to the US, not least because of its control of over a quarter of all known world oil reserves, that any talk of withdrawal of US forces would be strongly resisted. To withdraw would send a powerful signal that the US is not welcome in the region as a whole, and that al-Qaida had won a significant victory after the atrocities of 11 September.

Defence begins at home

In the United States itself, the Defense Budget for Fiscal Year 2003 (actually October 2002 to September 2003) is expected to increase by $48 billion, close to one and a half times the entire UK defence budget. This is the largest increase for more than 20 years and reverses many of the cutbacks achieved in the early post-Cold War years of the 1990s. Much of the increase will be accounted for by spending on homeland defence, together with spending on more precision-guided weapons and on missile defence.

Meanwhile, the Pentagon is trying to assess the need for maintaining current air defence patrols over US cities. Prior to 11 September, the North American Aerospace Defense Command (NORAD) maintained just 14 fighter aircraft at a high alert status, a number that surged to over 100 in the immediate aftermath of the New York and Washington attacks, and then doubled again within 24 hours.

Since then, numbers have decreased; but there are still combat air patrols mounted over New York and Washington. The patrols are supported by AWACS (Airborne Warning and Control System) aircraft, provided partly by NATO, as well as specific patrols to provide protection to President Bush and Vice-President Cheney when they travel outside Washington. By mid-January around 9,500 air defence sorties had been flown since 11 September, supported by 3,500 tanker movements.

The USAF patrols are provided partly by serving troops but partly by air force reservists, and the pressure of use is severely stretching their capabilities, both in terms of crew availability and maintenance of the aircraft. The problem is that the traditional 'threat' was always expected to come from outside. The head of NORAD, USAF General Ralph E. Eberhart, was quoted recently in *Aviation Week*:

> Regrettably, the threat to our air sovereignty can originate inside North America, as opposed to outside. I believe that has caused us to rethink the command and control, sensors and information that will be needed to perform our mission in the future. It obviously accelerated the requirement to move toward some kind of homeland defense command. The need is here, now.

America and the world: an abyss of perception
5 February 2002

As US military action continues in Afghanistan, the interim head of state, Mr Karzai, pleads with western states to extend the security assistance force to more of the country. The International Security Assistance Force (ISAF) has the capabilities to help maintain order in Kabul and the immediately surrounding areas, but would need to be many times larger to bring any degree of stability to the country as a whole.

To be fair to the Blair government, the UK has been quite generous, both with its troop commitments to ISAF and its programme to aid civil reconstruction. But few other states are making substantial contributions. The United States, having ousted the Taliban regime, is conspicuous by its silence and lack of support.

Meanwhile, warlordism and banditry are rife. Last week saw a bitter fight claiming at least 50 lives, as rival warlords fought for control of the town of Gardez in Paktia Province, just 80 miles south of Kabul.

Refugee movements continue, mainly as a result of people trying to get away from crime and lawlessness and aid agencies are having continual difficulties in moving supplies out of the major towns, as local transport routes are subject to looting and delays.

The State of the Union, and of the world

In the longer term, the other notable recent development was the State of the Union Address by President Bush, and its extraordinary divergence from the attitudes in most of the rest of the world. The Address, widely supported across most sectors of opinion in the United States, was blunt in its message of an ongoing 'war on terror'.

As US forces begin to operate in the Philippines, and bases are consolidated across Central Asia, so the message is clear: the United States will act wherever it thinks necessary, and has singled out Iraq, North Korea and Iran for particular attention.

While President Bush made clear his expectation that other allies would co-operate with the US, some of his most influential associates have confirmed that the US is fully prepared to act alone. At an international security conference in Germany over the weekend, Richard Perle said that the US had 'never been more willing, if necessary, to act alone'.

Earlier, and at the same conference, the US Deputy Defense Secretary, Paul Wolfowitz, had made it clear that US military policy was likely to be to pre-empt the acquisition of weapons of mass destruction by some states. He commented that since the 11 September attacks, 'we have acquired a visceral understanding of what terrorists can do with commercial aircraft'. He added: 'We cannot afford to wait until we have acquired a visceral understanding of what terrorists can do with weapons of mass destruction.'

Within the Middle East, reaction to this and similar sentiments is influenced, in part, by the knowledge that Israel has a formidable arsenal of nuclear weapons, and may have chemical and biological weapons as well. While Israel is seen in the United States as a close and trusted ally, it is perceived in the region as having a government which is more hawkish and repressive than any since the State of Israel was established in May 1948. The consequence of this, and other regional factors, is that there is an abyss between US perceptions of its security interests and those on the Arab (and Persian) 'street'.

Such a lack of understanding may be readily dismissed in Washington as of little or no account, given the overwhelming military strength of the United States and the continuing shock over the vulnerability demonstrated by 11 September. This, though, is a dangerous policy, not least because it is precisely the attitude that a group such as the al-Qaida network actively wants.

Given that the 11 September attacks were so well thought-out and planned, they demonstrated a sophisticated capability for developing a long-term strategy. A part of that strategy was almost certainly to induce in the US a fear of vulnerability that would ensure a very strong military counter-reaction. This, in turn, would lead to a further anti-American mood leading to more support for al-Qaida and allied groups.

For such groups, the State of the Union Address must have been like a dream come true. Not only is President Bush advocating a 'war on terror' that seems to be unmistakably concentrating on the Islamic world, but the United States is actually reinforcing its support for Israel, at a time when Israel's actions against the Palestinians in the occupied territories become progressively more rigorous.

The mood of the majority

In the longer term, it may be even more significant to examine the attitudes of opinion formers beyond the Middle East, in the 'majority world' of the south. Here, whether in the views of independent analysts or the private opinions of government officials, there is also a radically different approach to that in Washington.

It was expressed early on, in a perceptive comment on 11 September, written soon after the attacks by Walden Bello of the University of the Philippines. A paper on 'The Never Ending War', published by one of the most original and stimulating south NGOs, Focus on the Global South, condemned the attacks as horrific, despicable and unpardonable, but cautioned against an automatic 'iron fist' response that ignored the underlying context.

Bello pointed to the frequent use of indiscriminate force by the US, not least in Vietnam, and to the bitter mood throughout much of the Middle East and South-west Asia, directed partly at the United States because of its perceived dominance of the region but also against autocratic states dependent on continuing US support.

The analysis concluded:

The only response that will really contribute to global security and peace is for Washington to address not the symptoms but the roots of terrorism. It is for the United States to re-examine and substantially change its policies in the Middle East and the Third World, supporting for a change arrangements that will not stand in the way of the achievement of equity, justice and genuine national sovereignty for currently marginalized peoples. Any other way leads to endless war. (www.focusweb.org)

A more recent report from the South Centre in Geneva, sums up the mood among many southern opinion formers. The 'war against terror' is seen in the context of a widely perceived northern dominance of the international financial institutions, the tardy and thoroughly limited progress on debt relief, the general decline in aid budgets and a resolute opposition to trade reforms geared specifically to encourage southern development:

> Increasing numbers in the South perceive the evolving situation as no less than modern imperialism, using the full panoply of mechanisms to bend the will and shape the global order to suit the preference and need of the major advanced industrial nations. Moreover, this new imperialism is largely unhindered, in fact it is even aided and abetted, by the multilateral mechanisms developed over the past five decades.
>
> Growing resentment in the South at the sense of powerlessness in the face of Northern arrogance and impunity breeds frustration, which hardly provides fertile ground for development or peace or building the international community. Now, the fear of speaking up in defence of one's own interests has been further exacerbated by the new dictum 'You are either with us or against us'. (*South Letter*, 3/4, 2001)

These are two of many examples of attitudes across the majority world that could be drawn from newspaper editorials, magazine articles or radio and TV discussions, yet would go unrecognised in the current mood in Washington. The US sees the legitimacy of a 'war on terror' born of the shock of its own vulnerability. Much of the rest of the world sees it as a further example of the control of the international system by an elite minority.

The contrast is fundamental and may lead to an international dynamic that is deeply unstable. In between lies some independent analysis in the United States, and a much stronger current of concern within Europe. That concern is expressed more openly in countries such as France and Italy rather than Britain.

Tony Blair sees Britain as playing a bridging role between the United States and Europe on this and other issues. This is a view that is hardly shared in Europe, where the UK is seen perhaps more as a Trojan Horse rather than a bridge, but, in any case, Britain is not hugely significant in the wider scheme of things.

A difference of outlook on international security between the US and Europe is a matter of concern, but it is far less important than the wholesale fracturing between current US attitudes and those of the majority world. Perhaps what is really important in the coming months is for Europe to play a bridging role between the United States and the rest of the world.

War after war
13 February 2002

This series of articles has argued in recent weeks that the nature of the United States's bombing campaign will inevitably have caused substantial civilian casualties, and that media reporting has been so restricted that accurate details of the development of the war are slow to emerge.

In the light of current reports, both points are being shown to be uncomfortably accurate. This indicates substantial problems for the US in Afghanistan.

On the question of casualties, one of the most cautious estimates from a US source is from the Boston-based Project on Defense Alternatives. PDA, drawing on western media reports, concluded that over 1,000 civilians have been killed by the bombing and several thousand more have died from hunger, disease or exposure as an indirect result of the war.

Other estimates of casualties are much higher – certainly over 3,000 killed by the bombing. But it is probable that many of the deaths remain unreported because of the remote locations of many air raids and Special Forces operations.

What is clear is that there have been some serious errors by US forces leading to specific instances of substantial civilian deaths.

These have been compounded by the severe winter weather which makes it difficult for them even to determine the effects of some of the attacks.

What is becoming clear is that Hamid Karzai's interim administration in Kabul is coming under internal pressure to rein in the US activities, although this is highly unlikely to have much effect.

Other indications, from both US and Afghan sources, suggest that the manner in which the Taliban militia withdrew from areas of conflict and returned to their own home areas means that they have the capability to regroup. It appears that this is already happening, even during the winter months. In some areas, former Taliban have integrated into local ruling groups, and there are also indications that they are re-forming units outside Afghanistan.

A key area is eastern Afghanistan, where local Pashtun militia are refusing to co-operate with US Special Forces as they attempt to uncover Taliban and al-Qaida facilities and units. Given the risk of ambush, and the weather conditions, the US is reluctant to put Special Forces into the area and so relies on aerial reconnaissance and attack, with all the risks of mistakes and further civilian casualties.

To make matters worse, lawlessness and disorder are affecting much of the country. The UN Special Envoy, Lakhdar Brahimi, has urged a major expansion of peacekeeping operations. Brahimi is widely regarded as one of the most able diplomats in UN service, with a long record of work in Afghanistan. His confirmation of the need for a level of peacekeeping that far exceeds the work of the small ISAF force in Kabul indicates the extent of the problem facing Karzai's administration.

While further US military action in Afghanistan is inevitable, the pace may be slower for the time being, partly because of the weather and partly as a result of the evident errors that are being made. More generally, though, it is increasingly clear that the war itself has disrupted rather than destroyed the al-Qaida network.

Recent warnings of further attacks come on top of an FBI assessment at the end of last year that the network had had its capabilities diminished by no more than 30 per cent. Even by the beginning of February, it was reported that 16 of the top 22 al-Qaida leaders were still free.

Iraq – the next target?

Meanwhile, there are indications that the US war on terror is starting to move towards an attack on Iraq at some time in the next few months. A long-time feature of the rhetoric from the more hard-line security advisers in Washington has been the concern with Iraq and the determination to 'finish the job' by ending the Saddam Hussein regime. For the past five months the US has been preoccupied with Afghanistan, but Iraq was never far from the agenda and there have been signs of a preparation for action for several weeks.

One indication was the establishment of a US Army headquarters in Kuwait, this being part of the army's commitment to US Central Command (CENTCOM). There were also reports that elements of five army divisions, including some with recent desert training experience, were being deployed to the Gulf.

CENTCOM is the unified military command that covers the whole of South-west Asia, the Middle East and North-east Africa, and is the command responsible for the war in Afghanistan. If an attack on Iraq was planned, then it would be the responsibility of CENTCOM to carry it out.

These indicators of a potential conflict are countered by a report from the CIA last week that there was no evidence that Iraq has been engaged in direct terrorist attacks against the United States. At the same time, the CIA maintains the high level of US concern that Iraq has continued to develop biological and chemical weapons and long-range missiles since the ending of the UN inspection process nearly four years ago.

Two other factors need to be taken into account. One is that the US armed forces have used very large quantities of specialised munitions in the war against Afghanistan, running down stocks to the point where supplies had to be transferred from stocks in the Gulf where they were intended for possible use against Iraq. The past three months have seen intense activity among US armaments companies as the stocks are replaced and further supplies produced. This means that any kind of attack on Iraq would not be very likely until March or April at the earliest.

Secondly, the Saddam Hussein regime has recently made overtures to the United Nations, primarily on the issue of sanctions, but with indications that some kind of modest inspection regime might be possible. This could either be an attempt simply to ease the effects of the sanctions, or it could be a more calculated move to make it less easy for the United States to take any action against the regime.

What is more significant is the US response to this, especially as it came from a relative moderate in the Bush administration, Secretary of State Colin Powell. His immediate reaction was that the only issue was the necessity for an immediate resumption of inspections – nothing else was relevant in the short term.

More significantly, last Wednesday (6 February) Powell gave evidence to the House of Representatives International Relations Committee in which he confirmed that strategies to oust Hussein were under consideration and that the US 'might have to go it alone'. He went on: 'The president is determined to keep this on the front burner and is looking for options that are available to him to deal with this in a decisive way.'

This does not mean that an attack is imminent, certainly not one involving an open attempt to destroy the regime. That would take a massive build-up of military force in the region and there would be clear signs of this in advance. There is one option, though, that is certainly possible and would most likely play out in the next three months.

The first step would be a categorical insistence by the United States that the Iraqi regime accept a full process of UN weapons inspection pitched particularly at the biological, chemical and missile programmes.

If there was no response, an ultimatum of some kind might be given, with a fixed date for a response, in the near certain knowledge that the regime would not comply. There would then follow a major air assault on all the known Iraqi weapons sites and on the key Special Republican Guard and security units that ensure the maintenance of the regime.

While of a fixed duration, such an assault would be followed by a longer-term aggressive war of containment, aiming primarily at the core of the regime, and intended to last for months, certainly through until the mid-term congressional elections.

The Bush administration would make it clear that this was a process of constraining part of the 'axis of evil', so as not to heighten expectations of the early fall of Saddam Hussein. It could certainly be represented as a further major battle in the 'war on terror', and proof positive that the United States is determined to maintain control. Its possible effect on the mid-term elections in November would, of course, be purely co-incidental.

A major attack on Iraq is fraught with danger. The one issue that transcends everything else for Saddam Hussein is regime survival, and his military were prepared to use biological and chemical weapons in 1991 if an attempt had been made to destroy the regime. The same applies now, and any substantial attack on the regime has hugely worrying implications, not least because of the uncertain factor of the notably hard-line Sharon government in Israel.

The new military budget

Meanwhile, the new military budget has been announced for Fiscal Year 2003 (i.e. October 2002 to September 2003), and is expected to have an easy ride through Congress. The increases are staggering, and match the kinds of increases more common during the Reagan years of the early 1990s.

The 2001 budget was originally pitched at $298 billion – nearly ten times the size of Britain's defence budget – but eventually ended up at $315 billion. The 2002 budget started at $328 billion but was hiked up after 11 September by another $3.5 billion and will now rise by an estimated $20 billion to give an eventual figure of $351 billion. The 2003 request shoots that up to $379 billion. This means that the original figure for 2001 has gone up by $64 billion in two years – almost double the size of Britain's entire defence budget.

There will be many gainers, some of them stemming directly from the Afghanistan War. One obvious example is a rapid increase in funding to $141 million for unmanned combat aerial vehicles (UCAVs) – the pilot-less drones that can now carry missiles, together with $300 million to counter biological attacks and a substantial $9.2 billion for missile defence research.

In a true sign of the post-Cold War era, four Trident ballistic missile submarines will have their nuclear-armed missiles stripped out and replaced with 150 conventionally armed Tomahawk missiles for fighting 'small wars in far-off places'.

Some crude initial statistics on the extent of the war are coming out. It is currently costing about $1.8 billion a month. There are

4,000 US troops actually in Afghanistan and 60,000 in CENTCOM's overall area of responsibility, which stretches from Kenya across the Middle East to Pakistan. US aircraft have been dropping an average of 300 bombs a day since the war started.

A small but significant item in the defence budget is $98 million earmarked for increased support for the Colombian army in its war with left-wing insurgents. This will train and equip a Critical Infrastructure Brigade to help protect a 480-mile oil pipeline running from fields in north-eastern Colombia to the Caribbean coast. It may be a pure coincidence that the oil is owned by Occidental Petroleum, a US company based in Los Angeles.

A global war on terrorism

Perhaps the most significant indicator of an expanding war is the report that the CIA has extended its list of terrorist groups well beyond al-Qaida and its associates. As US action is stepped up in the Philippines, and there are indications of possible future action in Somalia and even Yemen, groups in Turkey, Lebanon and Colombia are now listed as posing a potential threat to the US.

The CIA Director, George Tenet, has identified Islamic Jihad, the Popular Front for the Liberation of Palestine and Hamas as terrorist groups, even though they have focused their actions on Israel. According to Tenet, 'If these groups feel that US actions are threatening their existence, they may begin targeting Americans directly' (*Washington Post*, 10 February 2002).

Tenet also lists the Revolutionary Armed Forces of Colombia (FARC) as another threat, even though it has not so far targeted the United States or even Americans abroad. The reason is that it 'poses a serious threat to US interests in Latin America because it associates us with the government it is fighting against'. Given the support that the United States is now providing for the Colombian government, that is a reasonable conclusion. But it does illustrate the manner in which the war on terror is becoming a global phenomenon.

Putting all of these elements together, we have a substantially increased defence budget, warnings of further attacks, a widening war against perceived terrorist groups and the prospect of a confrontation with Iraq. Afghanistan may have receded from the headlines but the reality is of a situation that is slowly but surely developing into a widening conflict with global implications.

4

Consequences of War

The early part of March 2002 was a period of key developments, all foreshadowing major conflicts and crises that were to come. In Israel, the failure of the Sharon government to control the Intifada, coupled with the continuing problem of Palestinian attacks within Israel, was causing the Israeli military to develop a far tougher approach in the suppression of Palestinian protests. In this process, it was aided by a belief in the Bush administration, supported by a perception within US domestic opinion, that the Israeli experience of suicide bombings was analogous to the 9/11 attacks. As a result, Sharon felt under little pressure from Washington in the pursuit of his more aggressive policies.

In Afghanistan, there was a major flare-up in the continuing conflict between US troops and guerrilla forces, much of it centred on Operation Anaconda, a military engagement that cost the Americans unexpected casualties. Furthermore, the renewed problems in Afghanistan came at a time when there were the beginnings of a perception of overstretch for the US armed forces. This came partly from the extension of bases into Central Asia, together with increased assistance for governments in countries such as Colombia and the Philippines. While defence budgets were set to rise, most of the new spending would be going on a combination of new weapons and equipment, coupled with improvements in pay and conditions for service personnel, rather than increases in numbers.

Even so, this was far from enough to convince the hawks in the administration that they should be more modest in their aims. With President Bush's domestic popularity still strong in spite of the Enron and Worldcom scandals, the belief was that the implications of US security policy should be followed through, with an increased emphasis on the requirement to terminate the Saddam Hussein regime in Iraq.

The coming war with Iraq
20 February 2002

In the past few days there has been a marked increase in the rhetoric about destroying the Saddam Hussein regime. It is coming from sources close to the heart of the Bush administration and is beginning to reach a level where to do nothing would be seen as a failure.

One part of the context for this is that there is a general perception that the war in Afghanistan has been won, that the al-Qaida network is dispersed and the Taliban destroyed. Whatever the reality on the ground, this is feeding a belief that more substantial wars can be won, and that the Baghdad regime, having survived since 1991, can now be overthrown.

There are three separate issues here. The first relates to motives for attacking Iraq and the second concerns whether such a war can be won. Perhaps most important is the final question – whether there could have been an alternative to the aggressive containment of the past decade that has resulted in so many problems for ordinary Iraqis while leaving the Saddam Hussein regime firmly in power.

Why attack Iraq?

One reason for going to war against Iraq is that this would be a key part of the 'war on terror', removing an autocratic and brutal regime that has been a consistent sponsor of terrorist actions against the United States. The trouble with this motive is that there is very little evidence that Iraq has done any such thing. The Saddam Hussein regime has certainly been consistently repressive towards its own dissidents, and has been ruthless in maintaining power, but a recent CIA report confirms that it has been careful to refrain from action against the United States or its facilities abroad.

The lack of evidence is certainly not for want of trying. There is a vigorous anti-Saddam mood in Washington with every effort made to find the 'smoking gun' – even the anthrax attacks last autumn were thought to have an Iraqi connection although the evidence now points to a domestic origin. Even so, the lack of a terror connection is not even remotely diminishing the determination to destroy the regime, so two other motives come into play.

One, obviously, is the extraordinary importance of Persian Gulf oil to the United States. The Gulf region dominates the world oil scene and provides the basic reason for the heavy US military presence there. When the Iraqis invaded Kuwait in 1990, they briefly controlled a fifth of the world's entire oil reserves. As was remarked at the time, if Kuwait produced carrots instead of oil, the Iraqis would not have invaded and the west would not have gone to war to get them out.

Saudi Arabia and the Emirates together hold half of all the remaining oil reserves in the world, and the presence of a regime in Iraq antagonistic to the United States is simply not acceptable to Washington.

Finally, and most significant of all, is the determination of Iraq to develop nuclear, chemical and biological weapons and ballistic missiles. From the Iraqi perception, this is an essential policy as it would provide a deterrent to US or Israeli intervention. There has consequently been a persistent process of maintaining a research, development and production capability right through the immediate aftermath of the 1991 war and the UN inspections in the early and mid-1990s.

The UN was pretty successful in dismantling most of the Iraqi nuclear programme and the more powerful ballistic missiles, and many tons of chemical weapons were destroyed. Some residual missile capabilities may still be intact, though, as well as supplies of some of the more advanced nerve agents such as VX. Far more significant is the status of the Iraqi biological weapons programme. This, together with chemical weapons and some delivery systems, has been an area of intense work in recent years, especially since the ending of the UN inspection process nearly four years ago.

The end result is that there is an assured belief in Washington that Iraq has weapons of mass destruction. This is, bluntly, unacceptable to the Bush administration in its current mood, so the Iraqi regime has to be destroyed.

From the perspective in Washington, this would remove an immediate threat to US security in the region, but it would have an additional longer-term benefit. Terminating a regime that is antagonistic to the US *and* has weapons of mass destruction would demonstrate unequivocally that the United States will not allow such a circumstance, and is prepared to use considerable force against any such state. In other words, destroying the Saddam Hussein regime is seen as a deterrent to any other state that is similarly minded.

Can a war be won?

The next issue is whether a war against Iraq can be won. Is it actually possible to bring the Saddam Hussein regime down by military action? The short answer is yes, but many Iraqis would be killed, the risk of escalation to weapons of mass destruction would be high, and the regional consequences could be immense. Even so, none of these seems likely to be sufficient to deter Washington in its present mood.

The Iraqi military are weakened compared with their power in 1990, and the United States has a massive military superiority. The extensive and persistent use of air attacks would eventually degrade the Iraqi armed forces, and might well lead to the capitulation of the regime. In the process, and remembering the US determination to minimise its own casualties, there would be heavy loss of life on the Iraqi side. Their armed forces would be subject to repeated area bombing, including the use of area impact munitions such as cluster bombs and fuel-air explosives, but the manner in which they would have dispersed themselves into civilian areas would ensure substantial non-military casualties.

The current US 'way of war' is far less precise than we are given to believe, as shown by the mounting evidence of thousands of people having being killed in Afghanistan. The same would apply to Iraq, but this is a country which, in spite of the eleven years of sanctions, still has effective military forces. As a consequence, the levels of attack employed by the United States would be much greater and more sustained than in Afghanistan.

There may be a presumption that the effect of such sustained attacks would be to demoralise Saddam Hussein's elite troops, ensuring that they turn against him and leading to the self-destruction of the regime. This might be so, but there is an alternative analysis that deserves consideration. Over the past ten years, the regime has survived sanctions and aggressive containment as a result of two factors. One is that it has gathered around itself substantial forces that have been doing rather well for themselves. Iraq, at present, has an elite of up to 1 million people, made up of the leadership and its supporters and the security and intelligence organisations, core elements of the armed forces and their families.

The second factor is that legal and illegal oil sales have been sufficient to bring in substantial resources, not least because some of the surrounding countries have done little to prevent smuggling. After all, why should countries such as Syria and Iran aid the United States in its war on Saddam when they could be, or even are, part of the 'axis of evil'?

The end result has been an acceptable lifestyle for the Iraqi elite, with the remaining 20 million Iraqi people experiencing constant hardship. The point is that this very elite has a huge vested interest in seeing the Saddam Hussein regime survive. It is therefore unwise to assume that they will turn on him, even under sustained attack from the United States.

There is a further issue that is particularly uncomfortable as the prospect of war looms. The Iraqis rapidly weaponised biological weapons at the time of the Gulf War, and were ready to use them had the regime been threatened directly with destruction.

While much of their nuclear and missile capability was destroyed during the 1990s under UN supervision, there is every indication that they have been working hard to develop effective biological and chemical weapons, and delivery systems. Any attempt to destroy the regime *must* be expected to result in the use of such weapons. If they were effective, either against US troops or targets in Saudi Arabia, Kuwait or Israel, then a nuclear response would be likely. This is a harsh reality that must be faced in any analysis of the consequences of a war with Iraq.

What has to be appreciated is that the fundamental motivation on the Iraqi side is regime survival, and it will go to almost any lengths to ensure this. If the regime is threatened with destruction then anything goes. In respect of this it is worth recalling aspects of the 1991 war that are conveniently forgotten.

Once Iraq had made the historic miscalculation of expecting a successful and sustained occupation of Kuwait after the invasion, it faced the build-up of overwhelming coalition forces, evidently sufficient to evict it from Kuwait. One key response, not recognised until well after the war, was that the subsequent Iraqi war aim was *not* to hold on to Kuwait but to ensure the survival of the regime.

Only two of the eight Republican Guard divisions were ever deployed near enough to the war zone to be engaged by the coalition forces. None of the Special Republican Guard forces appear to have been anywhere near the war.

These forces were kept well away from Kuwait and were available to protect Baghdad and the regime if the United States took the war into the heart of Iraq. What was an evident victory for the coalition forces in forcing Iraqi troops out of Kuwait, was also a victory of sorts for the regime, in that it not only survived, but was easily able to suppress the Kurdish and Shi'ite rebellions that followed the war.

There are further issues to be considered if a war with Iraq is planned. The Saudi regime will be hugely concerned with a domestic backlash as the US pours military forces into the region; and Turkey will be concerned that the destruction of the Saddam Hussein regime will lead to a fragmentation of Iraq, with the Kurds likely to unite with their fellow citizens in Turkey to create a genuine Kurdistan.

Moreover, the willingness of the Bush administration to back the policies of the Sharon government in Israel is seen from the Arab viewpoint as proof that repression of the Palestinians is a legitimate part of the self-declared war on terrorism. Whatever the validity of this view, it is a very strong perception in much of the Middle East. Indeed, we have to face the fact that an attack on Iraq would support the dominant view that the US-Israeli axis is deeply antagonistic to Arabs.

The long-term effects of such an attitude are difficult to predict. But the US military presence in Saudi Arabia has already been one of the factors that has lent such support to the al-Qaida network. In due course, another war with Iraq, with all the deaths that would result, combined with support for Israel, would certainly provide a powerful motivation for the further development of paramilitary groups intent on taking action against the United States.

Is there an alternative?

The most difficult question to answer is whether there is an alternative to current policies towards Iraq. There is certainly a very strong argument that another approach should have been tried during the 1990s – one comprising three elements.

The first would have been a much more substantial programme of UN food aid to ordinary Iraqis, a development of the food-for-oil approach that has existed in a limited form for some years. This would greatly have eased the malnutrition and health problems that have had such a bad effect, especially on children.

The second element would have been a much more sustained process of sanctions aimed specifically at the elite, including regional co-operation to limit the smuggling of oil that has served the regime so well. Targeted sanctions would have had to have been strongly supported regionally as well as outside the Middle East, and would have included tight control of financial transactions and a range of security related imports. It would also have involved controls directly aimed at the elite themselves.

The problem is that this would have been impossible to achieve without much better relations with several key neighbours of Iraq, which in turn required (and this is the third element) a sustained commitment to a fair and just settlement to the Israeli-Palestinian confrontation. This has not been forthcoming, except for brief periods in the 1990s, and the end result is that any attempt to have adopted this overall approach had little or no chance of success.

In any case, although this kind of approach has been advocated by many people, including former UN diplomats with significant experience in Iraq, it has proved unacceptable to successive US administrations. We are therefore left with a repressive regime that appears to be firmly in control, but with the great majority of Iraqis experiencing persistent hardship. The regime is now considered an unacceptable threat and must therefore be terminated.

Any attempt to destroy the regime carries considerable risks of escalation and of dangerous regional instability. Furthermore, large numbers of people will be killed in such a war.

It therefore makes real sense to investigate the alternatives. Such alternatives will be less easy to develop than five or ten years ago, and, for the moment, they will be dismissed in Washington as entirely unacceptable. This is no argument for not promoting them as an approach that contrasts markedly with the severe dangers and human costs implicit in a full-scale war.

European attitudes to 'the war on terror' are already in marked contrast to those in the Bush administration, both in relation to Iraq and in terms of attitudes to the Israeli-Palestinian conflict. It is just possible that influence could be brought to bear in Washington that would make the United States hold back from going to war, even as the preparations get under way. It is a role that Europeans can and should embrace.

The aftermath of war
27 February 2002

The situation in Afghanistan is becoming steadily more problematic. Regional warlords compete for power and influence, and the International Security Assistance Force (ISAF) is very much limited to Kabul. Hamid Karzai's interim administration is doing its best to bring a degree of stability to the county, and he has recently visited both Pakistan and Iran, but the problems facing him are immense.

There is continuing violence, especially in the south and east of the country, and there have been further movements of refugees across the border into Pakistan. The aid agencies had been hoping the opposite – that existing refugees would feel sufficiently secure to return to their homes.

One effect of the descent into 'warlordism' has been, as some analysts predicted, a sudden upsurge in the growing of opium poppies. They provide a ready source of income for impoverished farmers but, more significantly, opium production is seen as an essential resource by local warlords.

Ironically, the last year of the Taliban regime saw a ban on opium production, and the area planted with poppies fell by over 90 per cent. This is now being rapidly reversed and the street price of heroin in Western Europe is expected to fall within a few months.

Until recently, the United States was reluctant to get involved in post-conflict stabilisation in Afghanistan, leaving it to Britain and other ISAF contributors. Now, though, it is even being recognised in Washington that a deeply unstable and fragmented country will provide precisely the right environment for the Taliban to reappear and even allow some al-Qaida presence as well. For the time being, US actions may be limited largely to training a new central army for Afghanistan, but there are early indications that it might have to accept that large numbers of troops will need to be based there.

Of particular significance was the use of air power against warring militia groups last week. The bombing was not used against Taliban or al-Qaida units but against factions that opposed the Karzai administration, and took place near the south-eastern city of Khost. This was the first time, as far as is known, that the United States had taken sides in the latest phase of the fighting in Afghanistan. It suggests that a heavier involvement is already starting.

A slower build-up to the wider war

As the war on the paramilitaries expands, and the US Defense Budget grows, there is an assumption that the world's sole superpower has the ability to maintain and even enhance its military activity, with Iraq a likely target in the near future. Two particular features of military activity suggest otherwise, indicating that if Washington does intend to defeat the Saddam Hussein regime rather than just engage in further bombing attacks, this is unlikely to happen for several months.

The first factor is that the war in Afghanistan has taken a heavy, if largely unreported, toll on military equipment. A range of aircraft is being used at far above their expected utilisation rates. They include F/A-18 strike aircraft, F-14 interceptors and specialised intelligence and reconnaissance aircraft.

The requirements for airlifting large quantities of equipment and thousands of troops are putting a huge strain on transport aircraft, particularly the relatively new C-17. The sheer pressure of activities has resulted in a doubling of the accident rates compared with a year ago, with the air force, navy and Marine Corps all facing significant problems.

The situation is compounded by the need to maintain air patrols over US cities, even though NATO is providing AWACS airborne surveillance aircraft. It has also proved necessary to have aircraft on standby for domestic emergencies – the US Air Force is currently keeping some 35 C-130 Hercules transport aircraft on alert, draining resources from other tasks.

The second problem is that the US has been using a range of specialised weapons, especially satellite-guided bombs, at a rate far faster than they could be produced, substantially depleting stocks and making it very difficult to envisage a further major war in the next three months.

Armaments companies have readily moved into surge production, some setting up 24-hour production lines, but it will take up to six months before stocks of some weapons are considered adequate. So-called 'smart' bombs were being used at a rate of around 2,000 a month earlier in the war in Afghanistan. Yet even with the current expansion, production will not reach that level for many months.

At the same time, there are plenty of indications that the forces are starting to be built up for a confrontation with Iraq, with armaments companies reaping the benefits of substantial new contracts. Boeing, for example, is currently getting $30 million a month for producing the Joint Direct Attack Munition, a kit that converts so-called 'dumb' bombs into satellite-guided munitions.

The point is that the US military are feeling the strain of the Afghanistan War and the other elements of the escalating attempts to control paramilitaries. It will take time to develop and deploy the means to attack Iraq. This does not mean that it will not happen, far from it. It is just that the timescale is longer rather than shorter.

A possible timetable involves a tour of the Middle East by the Defense Secretary, Donald Rumsfeld, next month, followed by consultations between Tony Blair and George Bush in April. Some kind of ultimatum to Iraq on dismantling its weapons of mass destruction might be delivered in May or June, leading to a crisis and possible war later in the year.

The Iraqi regime could, of course, take a different view and some kind of conflict could develop much sooner. Furthermore, the situation is compounded by regional opposition to a new conflict. But this does not diminish its likelihood.

As George Bush has made clear, the 'war on terror' now extends to ensuring that states that are potentially hostile to US interests are not permitted to develop weapons of mass destruction. That is the bottom line in both in short and the long term, and it has clear implications for the Iraqi regime.

If all the indications are that the United States is determined to destroy the regime, but is not ready to do so, then one response is for the regime itself to provoke a confrontation soon. This would involve engineering a war at a time of its own choosing rather than waiting six months for the US to be fully prepared.

A global spread

Recent events in five other countries relate to wider aspects of the developing conflict. In the Philippines, the United States lost a helicopter and ten soldiers to unknown causes as it started its programme of putting in 600 Special Forces and support personnel to aid the Philippine government in its counter-insurgency action against Abu Sayyaf guerrillas.

Eighty of the 660 US troops are already in the Philippines. The helicopter was en route to Mactan Air Base, apparently returning from a deployment on the island of Basilan where the guerrillas operate. The United States has recently commenced intelligence-gathering flights over the southern Philippines, operating out of bases such as Okinawa.

US Navy planes have also commenced similar flights over Somalia, where P-3 Orion aircraft have been flying missions from a base in Oman. One of their roles is apparently to track the level of activity in presumed al-Qaida camps, to see whether the al-Qaida members who have left Afghanistan are now based there. If so, military action from the United States would follow.

In Colombia, where the government is due to receive increased US military aid, the cease-fire with the FARC guerrillas has been ended and there has been heavy bombing of rebel areas and attacks on the large enclave currently held by the rebels. The breakdown in the cease-fire follows the abduction of a government senator following the hijacking of a civilian aircraft last week.

The Colombian President, Andres Pastrana, is supported by the United States, which has now listed FARC as a terrorist organisation likely to threaten US interests. He has recently requested that US military aid provided to control drug production be diverted to counter-insurgency operations, and the new US Defense Budget includes substantial assistance in ensuring the security of a key oil pipeline. There are currently about 400 US personnel assisting the government in Colombia. The majority of them are military, but they include 100 'civilian military contractors'.

In Nepal, the Maoist rebellion has suddenly escalated, with substantial attacks in the western district of Achham, where 120 people have died, including police and soldiers. The insurgency is into its sixth year and has already claimed over 2,000 lives. Until recently, the Nepalese government has been receiving only limited help from the United States. It has requested much more assistance, given that the rebels have influence in some 40 per cent of the country.

Although links are claimed between al-Qaida and the Philippine rebels, there are no connections with FARC in Colombia or the Maoist insurgents in Nepal. Much more directly related to Afghanistan and the 11 September attacks is the movement of US forces into the unstable Caucasian state of Georgia. Last Wednesday, two US military aircraft arrived in the Georgian capital, Tbilisi, carrying around 40 US military personnel including Special Forces troops and logistic specialists.

The political background to this is significant. The Pankisi Gorge region of eastern Georgia has not been under government control for some years and has been used by Chechen rebels in their war against Russia. Georgia has been reluctant to co-operate with Russia in operations against these rebels, seeing it as a potential cause of greatly increased Russian influence.

Indeed, President Eduard Shevardnadze has been more interested in developing links with NATO. In the past couple of months, there have been indications that some al-Qaida forces have moved into the Pankisi Gorge region, and this has given Georgia the opportunity to develop closer military links with the United States.

For the US this presents a remarkable opportunity to extend its influence more firmly into the Caucasus and Central Asia. In addition to its deployments in Pakistan, it now has, or is establishing, bases in Tajikistan, Kyrgyzstan, Uzbekistan and Afghanistan itself. None of this will be readily accepted by Moscow, where the Putin administration has seen its influence in the region decline rapidly, even if it has been able to maintain close links with Northern Alliance members of the interim government in Kabul.

Pointers and postures

Some other pointers to longer-term developments are contained in the small print of the new US Defense Budget and elsewhere. During the Afghanistan War, the United States has made use of the AC-130 gunship first developed at the time of the Vietnam War. This version of the Hercules transport uses two cannon and a hugely destructive rapid-fire Gatling gun but the planes are getting old and the armed forces are now seeking a replacement. One possible device to be used in a replacement plane would be a directed energy weapon based on the development of the Advanced Tactical Laser.

Given the extensive use of the AC-130 in Afghanistan, such a replacement would be welcomed by US Special Forces, who are themselves getting a substantial boost in the new budget. The US Special Operations Command (USSOCOM) is getting a 21 per cent increase in its funding for the next financial year, taking it to $4.9 billion. Much of the addition will be spent on upgrading equipment that is being used in Afghanistan.

A further indicator is the Pentagon's plan to build up a force of some 45,000 guards and sentries to secure US bases overseas. This is in response to concerns over the security of such bases, arising not least from experience in the Middle East. There is a ready recognition that the US military presence may be singularly unpopular, and there have even been cases where bases have been relocated because of security concerns.

After the bombing of the Khobar Towers barracks block in Dhahran in 1996, the US moved its key air forces in the country to the Prince Sultan Air Force Base at a cost of $500 million. Although this base is in a remote part of the country, 10 per cent of the base personnel of 4,000 are concerned solely with perimeter security.

Finally, in the United States itself, more information is becoming available about the development of new types of nuclear weapon. The main interest is in so-called 'earthquake nukes', earth-penetrating warheads that can be used to attack deeply buried targets such as biological weapons stores that are too well-protected to be destroyed by conventional weapons.

The Nuclear Weapons Council has ordered a three-year study into such systems. According to the *Washington Post*, the administration has also established 'advanced warhead concept teams' at the three nuclear weapons laboratories, Los Alamos, Lawrence Livermore and Sandia.

Following the closure of many nuclear weapon production facilities in the 1990s, partly on grounds of safety, the Bush administration's Nuclear Posture Review now recommends accelerating development of a new plant to manufacture the plutonium cores of nuclear weapons. An additional $15 million has been allocated to enable the Nevada nuclear test site to be readied for further tests. These could be conducted within a year, although the administration remains committed, at present, to the current moratorium on nuclear tests.

It is now clear that the much-vaunted cutbacks in nuclear arsenals involve little in the way of irreversible dismantling of nuclear weapons. Most will be put into store and could be reactivated later. Furthermore, the Posture Review calls for initial work on a new intercontinental ballistic missile and a new submarine-launched ballistic missile. Any idea that the nuclear age is a receding memory is evidently fanciful.

The spiral of war
6 March 2002

There has been a tremendous escalation of the Israel–Palestine conflict, and, although unconnected, a regrouping of the Taliban. A number of recent aspects of both the Middle East and Afghanistan conflicts are both hugely costly in human terms, and also contain important pointers to the future. Some of the most significant aspects have been political. However, it is the military dimensions that may give us better clues as to the future.

In political terms, there are just the beginnings of a break in the bipartisan approach to the war on terror that has held so firmly in Washington. The Senate Minority Leader, Tom Daschle, has questioned aspects of its conduct. Admittedly, this is at a time when the public is starting to be prepared for an assault on Iraq which could come later in the year.

Yet even the modest breaking-away of Democrat support is significant. It may arise partly from a perception that President Bush's extraordinary popularity, which made criticism of the war so pointless, is starting to be affected by the corrosive nature of the Enron scandal.

The Middle East: escalation

In the Middle East, the Saudi peace proposal seems to have little chance of making progress, either in Israel or with some Arab states. Even so, it is an approach which focuses on one of the core issues, the occupied territories, while appearing to present the Saudis as more supportive of the Palestinian cause than has been apparent in recent years.

Within Israel, support for Sharon has declined. Most significantly, the 'refusenik' movement – of conscripts refusing to serve in Gaza and the West Bank – has grown in strength.

These limited political developments in Israel and Palestine come at a time of desperate violence, with the death toll rising in a series of bitter attacks by elements from both sides. Furthermore, there have been three developments that have caused real concern within the Israeli Army.

The first was the destruction of a Merkava main battle tank last month. Tanks have been a core component of the army's posture since the 1950s, and the Israeli Defence Forces (IDF) regard the Merkava as one of the most effective in the world. Yet, on this occasion, the tank was lured into a trap and destroyed, with its crew killed, by a crude explosive charge.

The second development has been the response of Palestinian militia to substantial Israeli incursions into refugee camps in Gaza and the West Bank. These were intended to clear parts of the camps believed to be used as home bases for militia, and the intention was to enforce the evacuation of sections of the camps prior to searching and destroying those buildings.

In the event, residents refused to obey Israeli orders to evacuate. Intense fighting ensued between Israeli troops and Palestinian militia. The immediate effects of such actions were that militia, civilians and some Israeli soldiers were killed. But it is actually significant that the Israeli troops failed to take over the areas they had intended to occupy.

The development is deeply reminiscent of the Israeli siege of Beirut in 1982 that led to a heavy loss of life, especially among civilians, when Palestinian resistance proved far more effective than expected.

The third development, and probably the most serious, was the attack over the weekend on an isolated Israeli checkpoint by a sniper, who killed and wounded a number of soldiers and civilians in a carefully calculated attack before escaping.

It is possible that elements of the IDF will start to recognise that they are becoming steadily enmeshed in a war in the occupied territories that they cannot win. Palestinian determination is strong, and every attack against Israeli forces is reported almost instantly on radio and TV throughout the West Bank and Gaza, as well as across the whole region.

The various militia have a high degree of community support and the IDF are having to operate in refugee camps or across stretches of land with substantial Palestinian populations. While many parts of the West Bank are rural, the majority is urban or semi-urban, and the potential for guerrilla warfare is high.

More particularly, there has been a long-term Israeli policy of locating settlements throughout the West Bank, not least as a means of ensuring that there cannot be the development of a viable Palestinian state. One result is that there is a huge network of roads that have to be patrolled in order to maintain the security of the settlements, with frequent checkpoints maintained in order to control movements of Palestinians.

In short, Israel has developed a system of close occupation of the territories that it regards as essential to maintaining control, yet this very system is being shown to be vulnerable to asymmetric warfare by Palestinian militia. Thus, the developments of recent weeks – the destruction of the tank, the sniper attack and the resistance to refugee camp incursions – may be more significant than the suicide bombings.

Furthermore, while the loss of life among Israelis, military and civilian alike, is increasing, the consequences for the Palestinians are far worse, with an economy in collapse, malnutrition in evidence, and a constant toll of killings.

Perhaps the core element in these terrible developments is that the resilience of the Palestinian communities shows no sign of diminishing, whereas there is a palpable concern in Israel over prospects for the future, demonstrated not least by the refuseniks.

It is possible that influential members of the IDF military command will be communicating to the government their concern over recent developments and may even be advocating renewed negotiations. It has to be said, though, that the nature of the Sharon government, and the pressure it is under from right-wing elements within Likud and in the wider coalition, means that the reverse is more probable – that even greater force will be used.

For the moment, too, Washington remains on the sidelines, with its characterisation of Palestinian militia as terrorists providing the Israeli government with a degree of support that makes a further escalation probable.

Afghanistan: unfinished war

For the past two months, the view in most of the mass media has been that the war in Afghanistan was over – that the Taliban had been defeated and the al-Qaida network disrupted. The leadership of both groups may have largely escaped, but all that was required was a crude 'mopping up' of small pockets of resistance.

A few other analysts and media outlets have taken a different view, and it is worth repeating that the Pentagon has always indicated that the war is far from over.

Despite public perceptions of an overwhelming Taliban defeat, the great majority of its militia withdrew from northern Afghanistan and from cities elsewhere in the face of US bombing and the rearming and support for anti-Taliban forces.

Moreover, Taliban militia withdrew with their weapons largely intact. With further supplies hidden throughout much of the country, they retained the ability to regroup in Pakistan. New leaders are likely to come forward.

Such an assessment also points to the probability that the al-Qaida network anticipated a strong US response to 11 September, and had few of its key forces even in Afghanistan. This, together with the escape of most of the Taliban leadership, is supported by what is known of the people currently imprisoned at Camp X-Ray in Cuba. They appear to be almost entirely made up of low-level militia and fighters, unable to yield much information and hardly representing any significant elements of leadership.

How does all this relate to the recent intensive fighting near Gardez in eastern Afghanistan, 100 miles south of Kabul and a long way from the traditional centre of Taliban power in Kandahar?

There are several elements to take into account. The first is the very straightforward one – that the US military have found it necessary to mount a very substantial operation, in very difficult high altitude conditions and in the middle of winter. They have committed at least 1,000 of their own troops, together with a number from other states, backed up by locally recruited fighters.

The Pentagon would only have even considered such an operation if there was firm evidence of a major regrouping of Taliban militia, sufficient to threaten US control at the end of the winter. This alone indicates that within Afghanistan itself, the Taliban have not just melted away into small groups spread throughout the country. They have been able to reassemble sizeable forces in the face of intensive US surveillance coupled with a constant capability to conduct bombing raids.

The second point is that the US has deployed regular troops in substantial numbers in direct combat roles, rather than the small groups of Special Forces used in the field up until now.

Moreover, these are army units rather than the more lightly equipped Marines so often used in the early stages of a war, implying that a longer-term involvement is now recognised as highly likely.

This is in marked contrast to the widespread political assumption that the United States would be 'in and out' of Afghanistan rapidly – destroying the Taliban and al-Qaida while leaving others to rebuild the state.

A third element is that the US is still endeavouring to rely heavily on locally recruited forces. In the current fighting, up to 1,000 such militia have been used, most of them receiving rapid military training and mostly paid directly by the US armed forces, the 'wages' being far in excess of what is available from the local economy.

In effect, the US is now using local mercenaries for as much of the fighting as possible, and is even avoiding putting finances into the hands of local warlords in return for the use of their militia. One obvious effect of this is to produce more people within Afghan communities who are heavily armed and have military training. A further possible effect is that they will embrace the mercenary role, being prepared to sell their services to others in the future.

Perhaps the most significant point stems from two related aspects of the operation near Gardez – that a significant proportion of the US force is actually being used to block exit routes for Taliban militia, yet that proportion engaged in direct combat has taken quite serious casualties.

In trying to analyse the events of recent days, we have to remember that information from the Pentagon, and from US forces in the region, is subject to extraordinarily strict controls. There is an almost complete absence of any independent verification of events, although some of the quality US newspapers are providing some relevant information.

What is clear, though, is that the US forces have had two helicopters subject to serious damage, have had some 40 troops killed or injured and have experienced a degree of resistance that was frankly unexpected. A report in the *Washington Post* (6 March) gives some indication:

> An opening advance on Saturday by Afghan and US Special Forces, intended to flush out suspected al Qaeda fighters in the town of Sirkanel, was thwarted when enemy gunfire kept coalition troops pinned down for hours. Elements of the 10th Mountain Division also were reported stopped in their tracks Saturday in a 12-hour battle outside the town of Marzak. Mortar rounds and rocket-propelled grenades landed as close as 15 yards to their position, and 13 American soldiers were wounded.
>
> 'I don't think we knew what we were getting into this time, but I think we're beginning to adjust,' said Sgt. Maj. Mark Neilsen, 48, from Indianapolis.

As the conflict developed, US capabilities had to be reinforced by five Cobra attack helicopters and two UH-53 transport helicopters flown in from an amphibious support ship, the *Bon Homme Richard*, in the Arabian Sea.

An unconfirmed report from the BBC suggested that the five helicopters were to replace a similar number damaged during the fighting. The fighting has involved intensive use of bombers, AC-130 gunships and thermobaric (fuel-air explosive) weapons, with 450 bombs dropped by US and French aircraft in the first four days alone.

There are now indications that few if any senior Taliban or al-Qaida leaders are in the area, and there may be very few members of al-Qaida even active at this time. What is clear is that a substantial force managed to regroup during winter, and that this has offered serious resistance to US efforts to maintain control.

What is not known is whether there are other such groups of a similar size and capability, or whether there are many much smaller groups spread throughout the country. This latter is at least possible, and knowledge of the original strength of the Taliban and its manner of dispersal suggests that there could be well over 20,000 militia available when spring comes.

The extent to which they try to regain control of parts of Afghanistan may depend on whether the interim government in Kabul can bring stability to the country. There are few indications that it will be able to do so.

Further extensive US military operations in the coming months may be more likely. Whatever else the past week demonstrates, it seems to confirm that the war in Afghanistan is far from over.

No end in sight
20 March 2002

Operation Anaconda was fought over two weeks in mountains near the Afghan town of Gardez. The effects of the battle are fundamentally disputed between the Pentagon and Islamic news agencies. The latter claim that a relatively small number of Taliban militia were able to hold out against far greater US and Afghan forces backed by intense air power, whereas the Pentagon view is that many hundreds of Taliban and al-Qaida troops were killed in a successful operation. There is no independent evidence available but there is a strong and perhaps understandable tendency in the western media to accept the US reports even if they may be open to question.

Whichever version is correct has important implications, not just for the war in Afghanistan but for the expansion of US military operations elsewhere. If the Pentagon view is correct, then there are only a few groups of Taliban and al-Qaida militia still active in Afghanistan and these will quickly be controlled by a combination of air power, anti-Taliban forces and some use of US ground forces, who will now be aided by a contingent of British troops. If the alternative view is right, then the United States could be in the process of getting involved in a substantial guerrilla war in Afghanistan that may limit its ability to take military action in other countries, including Iraq.

The background to Operation Anaconda

Before trying to make sense of the fighting near Gardez, there are several points to remember. In most of the fighting in Afghanistan over the past six months, there has been a consistent process of Taliban militia withdrawing, rather than engaging with anti-Taliban forces supported by heavy US air power. Very few of the Taliban or al-Qaida leadership have been killed or taken into custody – indeed it is still unclear how many al-Qaida fighters have even been engaged in the conflict. Those in custody at Camp X-Ray appear to be low-level people with very little information of real value.

Furthermore, the fighting near Gardez was widely reported as being the Taliban's last stand, but there have already been two earlier 'last stands', in Kandahar and at Tora Bora. In the first case, there was little fighting as Taliban militia withdrew, and at Tora Bora, several days of intense air bombardment did not prevent large numbers of militia withdrawing successfully across the mountains.

Perhaps most significantly, reports from western journalists travelling in southern Afghanistan indicate a degree of lawlessness and disorder, coupled with a rising anti-American mood in Pashtun areas, that suggests that support for the Taliban has not gone away but may only be dormant.

What, then, of Operation Anaconda? The operation was intended to destroy a group of several hundred militia located in high mountain areas above the village of Shah-e-kot. Unlike Tora Bora, the plan was to use many hundreds of US regular army troops, coupled with US and other Special Forces to surround the militia, while a combination of heavy bombing and the use of Afghan forces would lead to their defeat.

The operation began on 2 March after several weeks of planning, and was expected to last two to three days. There were initially estimated to be 600 fighters, mostly Arab and Chechen. Heavy fighting on 3–4 March left eight US soldiers dead and over 30 injured and a number of allied Afghan fighters killed and injured. Resistance from the guerrillas was much heavier than expected but 200 were reported to have been killed.

By 5 March, press reports were suggesting that there were up to 2,000 guerrillas in the area, either in caves or in surrounding villages. They were being bombed relentlessly and a local Afghan commander reported that they were low on ammunition and had become very weak. 'They can't escape. They're surrounded. Slowly we're pushing in.'

The following day, though, the US sent in substantial reinforcements including 200 more soldiers and 17 helicopters, having had seven helicopters damaged earlier in the fighting. It was now reported that local Afghans were joining the guerrillas in the mountains, even though 'hundreds' had been killed. A US general estimated that 600–700 guerrillas had been actively engaged in the conflict, about half of whom had been killed. The operation was expected to end shortly.

Over the period 7–9 March, bad weather limited the extent of the fighting, but there was an expectation that it would be over, with the defeat of the guerrillas, early in the week beginning 11 March, after perhaps ten days of fighting. Substantial additional Afghan forces were moved towards the area from Kabul and US sources now spoke of 500–600 guerrillas killed, almost as many as had been earlier estimated to be involved in the whole conflict.

Instead of the fighting escalating as reinforcements arrived, the US withdrew about one-third of the 1,200 troops from the area on 10 March saying that the fighting was largely over and would be continued by local Afghan troops. In apparent contradiction to this, local Afghan commanders reported only a pause in the fighting, prior to a possible final offensive within a few days.

There was no further major offensive and the fighting died down over the period 11–14 March. US sources described it as a 'mopping up' operation, with US and Afghan forces taking control of the Shah-e-kot valley. At this point there was a wide divergence between the US view of Anaconda and that of some local Afghan commanders allied with the US. The US view was of a substantial victory, with most of the guerrillas killed. One leading Afghan commander took the view, however, that substantial numbers of guerrillas may have successfully moved out of the area. There were also reports that some of those captured during the fighting were actually local farmers rather than guerrillas from other parts of Afghanistan or from abroad.

How many 'last stands'?

In a very confused situation, some tentative conclusions can be drawn. The first is that US forces met much greater opposition than had been expected. Given that the Taliban and al-Qaida were supposed to have been comprehensively defeated, it is clear that substantial guerrilla units had actually been able to regroup, and that US forces found it necessary to mount a major military operation in the middle of winter. The number of guerrillas killed is a matter of real dispute, with Pentagon officials emphatically rejecting the scepticism expressed by western journalists who visited Shah-e-kot after the fighting. Little evidence seems available to indicate substantial guerrilla casualties, certainly not in the hundreds. There have been further recent indications from local anti-Taliban leaders that many guerrillas withdrew successfully.

In an interview on 17 March, some two weeks after the operation started, the commander of US ground forces in Afghanistan, General Hagenbeck, remained optimistic about the outcome yet gave a clear indication that there would be further fighting involving US troops. His view was that many guerrillas, including their leaders, had been killed and substantial quantities of equipment and munitions had been destroyed, so much so that guerrilla forces 'will have to find new ways of supporting and equipping themselves'.

Even so, he continued, there would be further rounds of attacks on guerrilla units in different parts of southern Afghanistan, with intel-ligence-gathering planes focusing on two or three areas of potential activity. Perhaps most significant of all was the fact that he indicated some urgency because of a possible counter-attack. 'We think that there will be some groups that try to target American and coalition forces, looking for soft targets … We've got to get to them before they get to us.'

The implications of this are quite remarkable. After three 'last stands', guerrilla forces opposed to the United States in Afghanistan are considered to be sufficiently active and well-organised, even in the middle of winter, to be able to pose a threat to heavily armed US forces supported by overwhelming air power.

The United States now has some 4,000 combat troops in Afghanistan and appears to be in the process of getting sucked into a guerrilla war that may go on for many months. Bear in mind the degree of chaos and disorganisation in many parts of Afghanistan and, most significantly, that local Afghans may have joined guerrilla forces fighting in Shah-e-kot, rather than fled from them. It could be that we are seeing the development of a longer-term conflict.

'War on terror': slowing down or hotting up?

Strong support for this line of analysis is given by the US request to Britain to provide 1,700 troops from 45 Commando trained in mountain warfare. While part of the motivation may be to demonstrate that this is a coalition operation, the real implication is that US forces have found it so difficult to fight the guerrilla forces at high altitude that they require additional help.

There is also a political cost which has not been widely reported. Special Forces aside, the prime reason given for the British armed forces to be in Afghanistan was as peacekeepers in Kabul. In this way they would be seen to retain a more neutral presence, while the Americans engaged in large-scale combat. Now the British have lost this apparent legitimacy, as they too adopt an active military role.

Politicians can insist that the latter involves just the 'mopping up' of small areas of resistance, but their words simply do not square with General Hagenbeck's suspicion that Taliban/al-Qaida forces may be capable of offensive action.

If the General is right, and the war in Afghanistan stretches into the spring and summer, then the rate at which President Bush's 'war on terror' extends to other parts of the world may be slower than anticipated. This has considerable political implications as unease grows in Europe and outright opposition develops in the Middle East.

5

Israel and Palestine

During the course of April and May 2002, conflict continued in Afghanistan yet US resistance to expanding the International Security Assistance Force (ISAF) outside of Kabul was maintained. This left regional warlords to expand their influence, not least in allowing opium production to increase. There were also incidents involving al-Qaida, but the main area of crisis was an increasingly bitter confrontation between the Israelis and the Palestinians.

What began as apparently small-scale Israeli operations in the occupied territories evolved into a full-scale assault on the major towns and cities of the West Bank. In the process, several hundred Palestinians were killed and much of the infrastructure of the putative Palestinian state was dismantled by the Israeli Defence Forces.

Ariel Sharon was supported in his robust policies by large sectors of the Israeli population, not least because of the effects of the suicide bombs, but an added factor had been the immigration into Israel in the 1990s of around 1 million people from the former Soviet Union. They came seeking and expecting security, but found themselves opposed by an increasingly bitter Palestinian population; their reaction was primarily one of ready support for a hard-line response from Sharon.

The bitter confrontation, detailed in the following analyses, was made more possible for the Israelis by the reluctance of the Bush administration to condemn their actions, but one of its more important effects was to further damage Euro-American relations. For the most part, this was because so much of the infrastructure of the developing Palestinian administration had been financed and supported by states of the European Union and was now largely destroyed. There was also a wider recognition in Europe that an effect of the violence in Gaza and the West Bank would be further to alienate Arab opinion.

After many weeks of violence, there was eventually some slight easing in tensions but it later became apparent that strict military control of the occupied territories was extremely difficult if not impossible, in spite of the rigour with which the Israelis imposed their rule of occupation. In one sense, their problem was that their security posture had been largely predicated on defence against external threats, for which they were exceptionally well-armed, whereas they were essentially dealing with an insurrection from within.

Their eventual response, which began to become clear later in 2002, was to parallel their occupation, and the building of strategic settlements, with the construction of a massive wall that might eventually involve a physical separation of much of the Palestinian territories from the state of Israel. This later response, though, would eventually be seen as a tacit acceptance that indefinite military control of the Palestinians might carry a social and political cost that would be too great even for Israel to accept.

The widening possibility of war
3 April 2002

As Tony Blair prepares for his meeting with George Bush, the war in Afghanistan remains unresolved and the Israeli-Palestinian conflict worsens. Even so, the Bush administration remains intent on widening the 'war on terror' to Iraq, although the stresses being felt by the US armed forces are becoming more apparent.

It now seems possible that the British Prime Minister will counsel a degree of caution, but, while this might delay a US attack on Iraq, the more immediate crisis in Israel and the West Bank could rapidly extend to a wider war involving Lebanon and possibly Syria. Before addressing the logic of the momentous escalation in Palestine, we should consider the US engagement in Afghanistan which is currently slipping from the headlines.

Further conflict in Afghanistan?

As more information comes out of the Operation Anaconda episode in the mountains near Gardez, it becomes clear that few guerrillas were killed and most escaped to other parts of the country or across the border into Pakistan. Anaconda was intended to surround, and kill or capture a force of several hundred guerrillas, using over 2,000 elite US troops and Afghan allies supported by extensive use of air power. Even so, the guerrillas were able to inflict unexpectedly high numbers of casualties in the face of a carefully planned operation.

More recently, the Pentagon has made much of the capture of a senior al-Qaida operative, Abu Zubaida, in Pakistan. But he was not on the original list of 'most wanted' and may have been rather less significant than initially indicated.

Meanwhile, there are credible reports that Taliban militia are moving with impunity in the more remote parts of Pakistan. Many of the southern and eastern parts of Afghanistan are quite out of the control of the interim administration in Kabul, and US and other western forces are anticipating a drawn-out conflict, especially as spring comes. The official line of 'mopping up' Taliban remnants is strictly for public consumption. The reality is an expectation of a sporadic yet long-term guerrilla war.

This comes at a time when those few western reporters who have travelled outside of Kabul report a persistent anti-American mood, especially in the Pashtun areas.

Most indicative of this expectation is the decision by the US Air Force to base some of its A-10 ground attack aircraft at the Bagram Air Base in Afghanistan itself. This is the first time that fixed-wing strike aircraft have been based in the country and indicates an acceptance that there will be substantial further military engagement. The A-10 is the most robust and heavily armoured strike aircraft in the US inventory, and its basing at Bagram is a reflection of the difficulties US forces have had in using attack helicopters, several of their Apaches having been severely damaged in earlier fighting.

Military overstretch

There has been surprise that the United States requested help from Britain in the form of 1,700 troops, but this is in line with indications that US Special Forces are already under pressure. The essential reason for this is the heavy commitments that these forces have taken on in addition to their previous activities in many parts of the world.

Prior to 11 September, the US had counter-insurgency training and support missions in some 55 countries, with many of these drawn from the Special Forces. Since then, there has been intense activity in Afghanistan coupled with deployments across Central Asia, and in Pakistan, the Philippines, Yemen and Colombia.

Few reports of the effect of this activity are getting into the press. But there are indications that some of the limited numbers of specially modified helicopters and aircraft that are essential to special operations are becoming depleted through breakdowns or damage in combat. For example, two MH-47E modified Chinook helicopters were badly damaged at the start of Operation Anaconda and another crashed in the Philippines killing all ten people on board.

A key part of the Special Operations inventory is a heavy lift helicopter, the MH-53 Pave Low, with specialised equipment fitting it for this role. Three of the limited number of this aircraft have sustained considerable damage, others have received some damage and there is now a shortage of this type. Other versions of the MH-53 can be converted to the Special Operations configuration, but this takes time.

Overall, the US armed forces may be by far the strongest in the world, but they are becoming engaged in counter-guerrilla operations on such a wide scale that their more specialised forces are not available in the numbers required. Large numbers of reserves have been called up, and a feature of US newspapers is the placing of full-page advertisements for the US Navy and Marine Corps, seeking new recruits.

This does not add up to a long-term limitation, because there is ample evidence that the Bush administration is fundamentally committed to regaining and maintaining control, wherever US interests are considered to be threatened. Furthermore, the Defense Budget increases that are now envisaged will eventually deliver the forces required. In the short term, though, there are serious limitations and this is one practical reason why British troops are being sent to Afghanistan.

Israel, Palestine and Iraq

In any case, the sheer pace of the escalation in violence in Israel and the occupied territories is transcending immediate concerns about Iraq, although it may well have a profound effect on any such conflict later in the year. Vice-President Cheney's extensive visit to the region yielded little in the way of open co-operation. It is significant that US Central Command is moving some of its key command and control facilities out of Saudi Arabia and into the huge new base at Al-Udeid in Qatar, partly because greater co-operation might be expected from the Emir of Qatar than from the House of Saud.

What was impressed on Cheney repeatedly was the connection between Persian Gulf security and the necessity of controlling the excesses of the Sharon government in Israel. Although several key Arab leaders stayed away from the recent Beirut summit, it did herald the promotion of the Saudi peace proposals and also saw the partial return of Iraq into the Arab fold. Both of these are significant in the context of Arab attitudes towards Israel and the increasing, bitter anti-American mood in the Arab 'street'.

In Israel itself, the past two weeks have been traumatic, illustrating in a devastating manner the vulnerability of Israeli society to dedicated attackers who are prepared to die for their beliefs. In response to the attacks, the Sharon government has now embarked on a military campaign that is claimed to be designed to limit such suicide attacks but, in reality, has far more substantial aims.

As far as can be ascertained, there is no single central organisation responsible for the suicide bombings, but a dispersed coalition of units that may even operate independently. Such an entity cannot be dealt with by rigorous military operations – indeed the effect of such operations is much more likely to be to further radicalise Palestinian opinion. Moreover, the Israeli military and the security/intelligence agencies are aware of this and do not expect the current use of force to have such an effect.

What is actually happening is much more fundamental, and involves the systematic destruction of the Palestine Authority's security apparatus, including the civil police force, and much of the infrastructure of the PA itself. Many hundreds of officials have been taken into custody, offices are being destroyed, and the whole running of the PA is being curtailed if not eliminated. If the aim of the operation was to pressurise the PA into curbing its own militants, then it would require the PA to be able to do so. But the very forces that would be required to do just that are themselves being killed or taken into custody.

At some stage in the reasonably near future, the Sharon government may come under sufficiently heavy pressure for it to have to withdraw its forces. It will do so, under duress, but it will leave behind such a weakened PA that Sharon's longer-term requirement to have a series of isolated Palestinian communities with little central leadership will be easier to achieve.

We need to remember that the Sharon administration remains firmly opposed to the Oslo Accords and to the possibility of a viable Palestinian state. In this context, the current military operation seems specifically designed to destroy the short-term prospects for such a state. While that may be the intention, there is every sign that it is already proving to be deeply counterproductive. In recent days, Palestinian resolve appears to have strengthened greatly, and one effect of this is likely to be a further increase in bomb attacks within Israel itself.

That is unlikely to make much difference to Sharon's strategy, at least in the short term. The vulnerability felt within Israel, especially after the Passover attack, is such that Sharon retains sufficient support and Washington remains reluctant to intervene to urge restraint. The mood in the US remains broadly pro-Israeli and Sharon's actions against the Palestinians are seen as part of a process of homeland defence against terrorism. The idea of Palestinians defending their homeland gets little support.

Conflict in the north

There is one issue that may change the mood in Washington, and this is the prospect of a sudden extension of the conflict into Lebanon. From the perspective of the Sharon government, Jordan and Egypt present no threat to Israel – the two problems are the Palestinians and Hezbollah in Lebanon, the latter assumed to be backed by Syria and Iran.

There has been an increase in tension in southern Lebanon in recent days and it is possible that elements of Hezbollah militia may stage more substantial attacks on Israeli forces, not least as the impact of Israel's action in Ramallah, Bethlehem and elsewhere becomes apparent throughout the Middle East.

This, in turn, could be used by the Sharon government as a reason for engaging in substantial military action in Lebanon, including sustained air attacks in the Beka'a Valley. Such action would explain the otherwise puzzling decision to call up 20,000 reservists, and it would also fit in very closely with what is known about Sharon's own attitude to Israeli security. The implications for Washington would be profound.

If Israel were to end up engaged in a substantial war in Lebanon as well as within the occupied territories, then it would be far more difficult for the United States to consider taking action against Iraq. The regional reaction would be formidable – so much so that it might even lead to a degree of caution among those advisers in Washington who are so keen to see the end of the Saddam Hussein regime.

For many months now, the Bush administration has sought to separate the Israel–Palestine confrontation from its own intentions to extend the 'war on terror' to Iraq. That is now an impossible task and Tony Blair will do well if he can impress that on George Bush in his forthcoming meeting.

Israel's strategy: the impotence of arms
11 April 2002

As the Israeli military attacks on the West Bank continue, their full aim is becoming apparent. It fits in closely with Ariel Sharon's longer-term policies, has little to do with curbing suicide bombers, and has serious implications for the region as a whole and the security of Israel in particular.

It is probable that the entire operation was originally intended to take about four weeks, with rather more than half of that involving intense military actions in cities and towns throughout the West Bank. The climax of the operation would come with protracted assaults in Gaza, including the occupation of the densely populated Palestinian refugee camps.

There was an expectation that the United States would not intervene early enough to limit the full extent of the military operations, but this has been turned on its head by the intense pressure on Washington from a number of Arab states. The most notable of these have been Egypt and Jordan, not least as their own populations respond to the 'Al-Jazeera factor' – the widespread and persistent reporting of the Israeli actions on independent satellite TV news channels.

At the time of writing (10 April), large-scale military operations have not commenced in Gaza. If they do, then the fighting will stretch over at least a week and will be of an intensity exceeding that of

Nablus, Jenin and Bethlehem. It will be a disaster for the United States and will further inflame tensions across the Middle East.

However, if Sharon holds back from going into Gaza then his full intentions will not have been achieved. Moreover, Hamas, which draws much of its strength from communities in Gaza, will see its position enhanced within the Palestinian community.

Israel's real purpose

If one thing is well-nigh certain about the intense conflict of the past two weeks, it is that the purpose is not to curtail the risk of suicide bombing. That is not something that can be done by blanket military operations against centres of Palestinian population. Indeed it is very much more likely to produce further generations of potential suicide bombers.

The military operations actually have a quite different purpose, and this has become clear as the effects of the war have become apparent. They are, in short, aimed at destroying the capacity of a putative Palestinian state to operate.

Information on the impact of the Israeli attacks remains extremely limited, as journalists have been prevented from reporting from within the Palestinian areas, but some reports have seeped out. Firstly, it is probable that casualties have been high, with several hundreds killed on the Palestinian side, and many more seriously injured. Secondly, there has been a systematic process of dismantling the apparatus of the Palestine Authority.

Much of the military action has been directed against the police and security forces of the PA, with substantial numbers having been killed and many hundreds taken into custody. Police stations and barracks have been destroyed, as have intelligence and security centres. Moreover, and in some ways much more significant, there has been the destruction of the PA's administrative infrastructure.

Information on this remains incomplete but is sufficient to show that there has been widespread destruction of offices and facilities of PA ministries and Palestinian non-governmental organisations. The Ministry of Local Government and the Ministry of Education in Ramallah have been ransacked by Israeli troops, as has the Palestinian Bureau of Statistics.

NGOs engaged in medical support and youth work have seen their offices destroyed. Shopping centres have been damaged, electricity transmission lines and water mains have been destroyed, and thousands of houses have been wrecked or damaged.

None of this will directly limit the risk of suicide bombings, but it will certainly have a major impact on the ability of the PA to run its own services when there is a military withdrawal.

Overall, the Sharon policy is one of dismantling the apparatus of the Palestinian state that has been built up over the past eight years. Indeed, one of the significant if subsidiary reasons why there is so much anger in a number of European capitals is that much of this infrastructure has been carefully developed with aid from EU states and is now wrecked.

The Lebanon experience

The parallels with the Israeli military action in Lebanon in 1982 are highly relevant to current circumstances and give us some idea of the likely consequences of the current operations.

Sharon launched Operation Peace for Galilee on behalf of the Israeli government in the summer of 1982 in response to rocket and other attacks across the border from south Lebanon and in the wake of an assassination attempt against the Israeli ambassador to London. It was claimed initially to be a limited military operation designed to produce a secure zone in southern Lebanon: the war over the Falklands/Malvinas islands between Britain and Argentina earlier that year was cited as an example of the legitimacy of taking such action in pursuit of security.

In the event, it turned out to be the start of a massive military operation by land, sea and air designed to destroy the Palestinian military organisation in Lebanon. The invasion took the Israelis right up to Beirut and resulted in the hugely destructive siege of West Beirut, with more than 10,000 people killed, even before the massacres in the refugee camps at Sabra and Chatilla later in the year.

Poorly-armed Palestinian militia proved very difficult to overcome and international pressure eventually forced an Israeli withdrawal from Beirut that also involved the evacuation of Arafat and his militia to Tunis. The Israelis stayed in occupation of southern Lebanon for several years but eventually withdrew from much of the territory in the face of guerrilla actions by Hezbollah militia.

Resistance from the Palestinians in West Beirut was greater than expected, and one response by the Israeli Defence Forces was to make extensive use of artillery and air attacks. These were frequently deployed in densely populated urban areas – one of the reasons for the high number of deaths and injuries. Similar tactics are being used at present.

If the current operation was to continue to its planned completion, there would be little left of the PA infrastructure; yet if negotiations were to become possible, then the Palestinians would be placed in a real position of weakness. That, at least, appears to be the position of the Sharon government, and would result, in the government's expectations, in a settlement in which control of the occupied territories would remain firmly in Israeli hands.

Further suicide bombings would prompt further substantial use of force, and Palestinian entities would be limited to a number of weak centres of population heavily constrained by settlements, strategic roads and appropriate military control.

Three conditions of conflict

Although most international opinion remains deeply critical of the current Israeli operations, Sharon retains support within Israel, at least for this action, even if a substantial minority of the population would prefer the rhetorically more extreme Binyamin Netanyahu.

The main and obvious reason for this support is the deep-rooted effects of the suicide bombings on Israeli society, especially the Passover massacres. This is compounded by the outlook of around 1 million recent immigrants, mostly from Russia. Their presence has moved the Israeli political scene further to the right, not least because their own perceptions of insecurity are perhaps even greater than longer-established citizens.

There is therefore a combination of three factors. One is Sharon's own predisposition for hard military action and utter distaste for compromise. The second is the level of domestic support, and the third is the lack of any real pressure from the United States, even bearing in mind George W. Bush's recent statements. It will have taken Colin Powell seven days to make the twelve-hour journey to Israel, allowing the Israelis sufficient time to rush through their operations on the West Bank.

Israel threatened from within

There appears to be an assumption, within both the Sharon government and Israeli armed forces, that the current operation will suppress Palestinian aspirations and allow greater Israeli control. This is unlikely in the extreme. The Palestinians lost many thousands of people in Beirut in 1982, about 1,000 were killed in the first Intifada and another 1,000 had died in the uprising over the past 18 months. None of this destroyed their resolve to overturn occupation, and the current Israeli action is likely to strengthen greatly the more radical elements.

Recent perceptive interviewing by some western journalists with Hamas leaders in Gaza confirm that *their* analysis is that Israel is doing precisely what Hamas wants. The intense military action, killing and injuring very many hundreds of Palestinians, will serve to further radicalise opinion, bringing forward many more people willing to die for their beliefs. In all probability, there will be further and more extensive use of suicide bombings in the months ahead, as the bus-bombing in Haifa has already shown.

There are two further factors that should cause concern for anyone with the genuine security interests of Israel at heart. One is the widespread assumption within Israel that Palestinian society is composed of ill-educated religious extremists and that anyone who opposes Israeli troops in their actions is necessarily a terrorist. Nothing could be further from the truth.

Palestinians in the occupied territories are probably the best-educated people in the whole of the Arab world, with a remarkable network of schools and universities forming the basis of an intense concern with education. Not only are they very well-informed, and determined, but they have at least as great an attachment to their country as the average Israeli has to Israel.

The second factor is more ominous for the Israeli security forces. In the last two weeks of intense fighting, Israel has been fully dominant in its use of firepower, using tanks, artillery, bombers and attack helicopters with near impunity. Yet it has proved difficult and costly to take control of some of the Palestinian urban areas, as events in Jenin have demonstrated.

Furthermore, there is little evidence of the discovery of major arms supplies, and Palestinian militia have made little use of some of the more effective weapons that they undoubtedly have.

Sharon's very use of military force therefore results in Israel being in a huge dilemma. If the armed forces units are withdrawn from the main centres of Palestinian population, the militia will regroup, the suicide bombings will continue and they may well intensify. If, on the other hand, Israel maintains a high level of military occupation, it will not only fly in the face of international opinion, but its military forces will become persistently vulnerable to guerrilla attack, as was already starting to happen up until last month.

There is, for Israel, a very uncomfortable conclusion to be drawn from this use of force: as well as being tremendously costly in human terms, it will actually be deeply counter-productive to the security of the State of Israel.

In the final analysis, there is no alternative whatsoever to Israel negotiating a full and just settlement with the Palestinians. What appears currently to be the powerful and effective use of force by the Sharon government is actually disguising a deteriorating security environment for Israel and is the greatest obstacle to Israel gaining a peaceful and secure future.

An expanding horizon of conflict
17 April 2002

US Secretary of State Colin Powell's efforts to restrain Sharon have so far achieved no more than a tentative plan for a regional peace conference. Two suicide bombings and the underlying determination of the Sharon government to take the military route, no matter how counter-productive, have ensured that Israeli forces remain throughout most of the West Bank. How Sharon will act after Powell returns to Washington will give some indication of the extent of his determination, especially if he sends troops into Hebron and even into Gaza.

A wide swathe of international opinion across Europe sees Sharon's policy as potentially damaging to the State of Israel itself, further radicalising Palestinian and wider Arab opinion, especially as the extent of the damage and casualties in Jenin and other towns and cities becomes apparent. There is deep unease also in Jewish communities across the west, as concern over Sharon's harsh measures conflicts with worry for the future of Israel.

The extent of Sharon's support within Israel has caused surprise among many observers, but it comes within a context that makes it understandable, at least to an extent. Until recently, and with only two exceptions, Israel's many conflicts with the Palestinians and surrounding Arab states have caused few casualties to the Israelis themselves.

Can Israel win?

The first month of the War of Independence in 1948 was costly, but the war ended a few months later with the new state making substantial gains in territory. Suez in 1956, and especially the Six Day War in 1967, resulted in huge Arab losses at little cost, as did the invasion of Lebanon in 1982. In the latter case, Israel eventually withdrew from most of Lebanon, having lost 500 soldiers over a three-year period, but the Arab losses were more than 20 times as great.

Only in the Yom Kippur/Ramadan War of October 1973 did the Israelis sustain major casualties, and that was one of the factors that resulted in a political shift to the right and the access to power of Likud four years later.

In the past few months Israel has experienced repeated loss of life through individual shootings, ambushes and, above all, the suicide bombs. There is no direct way to counter the latter, and they have given rise to a degree of anxiety that is pervading the country. In part, this is because the hundreds of people who have died are drawn from a small country and the bombers strike at the heart of the major cities, but there is also the factor of the sheer unpredictability of the attacks, leading to a deeply unsettling mood.

The response, with Sharon in charge, hard-line politicians joining the cabinet and Netanyahu waiting in the wings, is a willingness to use force that comes from a single-minded political determination combined with a public mood that will back almost any strategy of force, no matter how deeply flawed and dangerous.

What is beyond comprehension in much of Israeli society is the effect of these actions on Palestinian society. After 35 years of occupation, the encroachment of settlements, the building of strategic roads, abstraction of water supplies, appropriation of land and all of the other features of occupation, the Intifada is being met with the destruction of Palestinian infrastructure, wholesale damage to dwellings and shops, and the deaths of well over 1,000 people.

This is in a population that is even smaller than that of Israel, that now has a standard of living much less than one-tenth of that of Israel, has rampant unemployment, and is experiencing a degree of control that is akin to a huge open prison. Even so, and based on past experience and recent information, all the signs are that the Israeli action will serve only to harden Palestinian resolve, to further radicalise opinion and produce many more thousands of young people prepared to respond with force.

Israel has a degree of conventional military power massively superior to that of the Palestinians, yet its very policy of settlements through the occupied territories means that it cannot retreat into a heavily defended heartland. It is therefore vulnerable to asymmetric attack that will result in a further cycle of violence.

In such circumstances, it is possible that domestic opinion in Israel will eventually turn away from current policies, but it is all too easy for Sharon to direct opinion towards further support for his military action. It may therefore be up to external actors to force a change, but there is little sign of the determination in Washington that would be required.

A new politics of extremism?

Perhaps Mr Powell's repeated experience of the anger expressed in the Arab capitals he has visited will have an effect. But that is unlikely unless European states are far more forceful in their dealings with Washington, or the Arab states decide to use their leverage in terms of their control over oil and the military facilities they extend to the US across the region.

Many years too late, the Saudi peace plan adopted by the Arab League offered unequivocal recognition of Israel and its right to exist if it withdrew from the occupied territories. Sharon promptly ordered his assault upon them, as if to declare that he had no interest in any peace authored by the Arabs but only one imposed by Israel itself.

But it may be that such an Israeli attitude relies upon the Arab states in another way: that they will remain pliant regimes of America's overall dominance in the region. However, Israeli intransigence and Palestinian losses may greatly increase the popularity and support for bin Laden-style anti-Americanism.

These weekly columns have consistently argued that al-Qaida has been seeking to provoke escalation from which it believes it will indeed benefit over time. Should the Saudi royal family feel genuinely threatened domestically by the appeal of bin Laden they may seek to outflank it by turning more forcefully against Washington. The Palestinians can hardly afford to pin their hopes on such a prospect, but a new politics of extremism in the age of globalisation may break open Arab societies whose closure has hitherto been essential to their weakness.

Afghanistan remains

Meanwhile, in Afghanistan, al-Qaida continues to regroup. Early last month, US Special Forces and Afghan allies staged Operation Anaconda, high in the mountains in eastern Afghanistan, near the town of Gardez. As the name implies, the intention was to constrict a substantial group of many hundreds of Taliban/al-Qaida guerrillas, capturing or killing them. In the event, the US forces suffered substantial casualties, the loss of two helicopters and damage to several more, and most of the guerrillas were able to escape.

Other features of Anaconda were that it had been planned for some time as a result of intelligence that the guerrilla forces were regrouping, and that they were joined by local people opposed to what was seen as western interference in their country.

Even so, the word from Washington (and London) was that this operation was no more than a 'mopping up' operation, part of a process of finally defeating the remaining Taliban and al-Qaida elements in Afghanistan. This contrasted markedly with the views of some independent analysts who were prone to point to the idea that the Taliban had, by and large, chosen to withdraw during the war the previous autumn, rather than face destruction by US air attacks and associated action by the Northern Alliance.

Such analysts also took the view that the Taliban had melted back into their own communities, either in Afghanistan or across the border in Pakistan and that there were probably very few al-Qaida fighters even in Afghanistan after 11 September.

The extent of the Anaconda action and the ferocity of the guerrilla attacks seemed to support this alternative analysis – if this was truly just part of a 'mopping up' operation, that it was trying to deal with a sizeable flood.

What was clear was that a more accurate indication of the extent of opposition to US and coalition control would be more likely to come with the onset of spring and summer. In anticipation of increased action, the US persuaded Britain to commit 1,700 troops, many of them Commando specialists in mountain warfare, and elements of this group started their military operations a few days ago.

This alone indicates perceptions of substantial problems ahead, with indications of a substantial increase in guerrilla activity in the east of the country. On 13 April, rocket-propelled grenades were launched against a US-controlled airfield near Khost, and there were further explosions the following night. A joint US-Afghan patrol had also come under attack on 13 April, following an earlier attack the previous day. Although there were no US casualties reported and five of the guerrilla force were reported killed, these actions indicate a resurgence of military activity.

What is perhaps much more indicative is that, in all four cases, it was the guerrilla forces that initiated the attacks, rather than responding to US 'mopping up'. Military spokespeople persist in claiming that there are no more than a few hundred guerrillas active in the whole of the country, but this seems implausible in the extreme.

A state of disorder

Over the next three months we will get a clearer indication of whether a longer-lasting guerrilla war is beginning to develop, but the early signs are that it is. Moreover, Afghanistan remains substantially in a state of disorder, despite the efforts of the Karzai administration. Attempted assassinations, bomb attacks, shooting at ISAF patrols and warfare between local warlords are all features of the current scene.

They indicate that UN estimates of the need for a stabilisation force of at least 30,000 can hardly be too many, but there is no political will to deploy such a force. The end result is a degree of instability away from Kabul that will make it much easier for Taliban units to operate, and much more difficult for any kind of unified government to exert control. In such circumstances, protracted military action involving US, British and other coalition forces should not come as any great surprise in the coming months.

Iraq and Palestine: two theatres of war
24 April 2002

Colin Powell returned to Washington last week having made virtually no progress during his convoluted travels across North Africa, Europe and the Middle East. President Bush's call for an Israeli withdrawal three weeks ago was ignored. But even this unsuccessful attempt to influence Ariel Sharon was enough to increase pressure on him from the Israeli lobby in Washington. This included a remarkably warm reception given to Sharon's representative, former prime minister Binyamin Netanyahu, by a cross-party group on Capitol Hill.

One of the reasons for the current influence of the lobby is the manner in which it has become possible to connect the attacks on New York and Washington with the bombings that have had such an effect in Israel. To a wide swathe of domestic US opinion, the Israeli action is perfectly consistent with America's war on terror, and this makes it so much easier for Israel to maintain support in the United States.

There may still be a certain diversity of opinion within Washington, with some experienced officials in the State Department much more conscious of the strength of Arab opinion and the risk of instability across the region. Even so, the administration remains firmly committed to Israel and even to the Sharon government's current hard-line policies. Israel remains the largest recipient of US aid, the 2002 programme including $2.04 billion in military aid and $730 million in other support, close to one-fifth of the entire US aid budget.

Iraq: still the eventual target

Although attention is currently concentrated on Israel, the longer-term aim of terminating the Saddam Hussein regime in Iraq remains very much on the agenda. Military action may not happen for many months yet, not least because of the need to produce sufficient quantities of specialised munitions, but forces are already being gathered in the region. It has now been confirmed that a substantial expansion of base facilities in Qatar and Oman is under way, one reason being that there remains a question mark over Saudi willingness to allow their bases to be used in any attacks on Iraq.

Another indication of the US policy towards Iraq is the success of the US action in forcing the head of the Office for the Prohibition of Chemical Weapons (OPCW) out of power. Jose Bustani of Brazil was regarded by the US as too supportive of the idea that Iraq might take up membership of the OPCW. If Iraq became subject to OPCW inspections, this would make it more difficult for the US to take military action later in the year.

Most analysts believe that, in the face of a likely US attack, the Saddam Hussein regime will appear to concede the need for UN inspections of its weapons of mass destruction facilities, playing out the process for as long as it possibly can. This would only delay, not prevent, a US attack. But the aim would be to enhance support across the region, making it more difficult for the United States to rely on assistance from neighbouring states.

There is, though, an alternative Iraqi strategy which would make war much more likely in the short term – even before the autumn. For the Saddam Hussein regime, the most important thing by far is regime survival, transcending all other political aims. If the regime is convinced that the Bush administration intends to destroy it, then it could well provoke a crisis that forces the United States to take military action long before it has the necessary forces to enable it to threaten the regime itself.

It is just possible that the current efforts by the Iraqis to upgrade their air defences might develop into a sustained process of infringements of the no-fly zone. This could happen within the next month, but might be more likely during the hottest time of the year in July. It would present Washington with a dilemma – either attack Iraq without the forces necessary to destroy the regime, or appear weak in the face of Iraqi provocation.

Iraq, in turn, could present its actions as legitimate defence, a tactic that would be readily accepted in much of the Arab world. It would come at a time when Iraq is gaining favour by its support for Palestinians, both through its embargo on oil exports and the monetary aid that it is feeding through to bereaved families and the newly homeless in the West Bank.

Sharon's fourth aim

At the start of Israeli military action in the West Bank last month, the official line of the Israeli government was that there were three aims. One was the isolation of Arafat involving the reduction of his status to the point where he became irrelevant. This was most noticeable in Sharon's talk of a 'one-way ticket' for the Palestinian leader. The second was to take into custody or kill those responsible for the suicide bombings that were having such an appalling effect on Israeli society. The third was to uncover and destroy the arsenals of weapons and explosives that supported Palestinian militancy.

While these were the stated aims, it quickly became clear that there was a further aim – the systematic dismantling of the security and administrative infrastructure of the Palestine Authority. As Israeli troops have withdrawn from some areas, the extent of this last aim has become apparent, with frequent and independent reports of extraordinary damage done to administrative centres. Furthermore, this has extended to support infrastructure including water and electricity supplies, roads and even sewers, as well as to radio and television stations.

One of the features of Palestinian life in recent years has been the growth in the number of such media outlets, part of a network of around 50 radio and TV stations throughout the occupied territories. Most of these are private, there has been relatively little in the way of censorship and they have helped to enhance a Palestinian sense of identity. During the recent occupation, many of these were occupied and then destroyed, including the majority of the six radio and six TV stations in Ramallah alone.

The destruction was specific and well-organised, with soldiers using sledgehammers to work their way through the studios and control rooms, systematically destroying the cameras, recording suites, control systems, computers and transmitters. Much of the equipment had been provided by government and private agencies from overseas, and its destruction will further damage Israel in the eyes of many organisations.

There has been a similar problem of the effects of behaviour in relation to the international media. Many individual reporters, sound recordists and camera operators attempting to report on recent developments on the West Bank have experienced considerable difficulties and, on occasions, violence, from Israeli soldiers, behaviour that will further lose them sympathy for their predicament from the international media.

The behaviour of the Israeli troops should not come as a surprise and stems from two main factors. One is the manner in which Israel has traditionally used very tough military force, including heavy weapons, in any circumstances where there is armed opposition, not least because it places a premium on the safety of its own troops. Sharon, with his particularly hawkish approach, has no problem with this tactic, indeed he encourages it openly to the extent that middle-ranking army officers know that they will not be limited by the attitudes of their superiors.

The second concerns the situation is which the young soldiers find themselves, especially conscripts and reservists. Although the Israeli army is extraordinarily powerful and well-equipped, it has faced determined and sometimes effective opposition from Palestinian militia defending their own homes and communities. Considerable fear and apprehension is present among the soldiers, few of whom have experience of urban conflict and guerrilla actions. There is, furthermore, no direct military answer to suicide bombings, just a constant concern that *any* Palestinian might be a threat.

The effects of Sharon's war

One long-term question here is what effect Sharon's actions will have on Israeli society. He currently retains strong support, not least because of the traumatic effects of the suicide bombings. But prior to the recent military action there was a growing movement of 'refuseniks'. They may be greatly strengthened by soldiers, especially reservists, who have first-hand experience of the behaviour of the army in Bethlehem, Ramallah, Nablus and especially Jenin.

Overall, the less obvious aim of the military action, destroying infrastructure, will greatly limit the ability of the Palestine Authority to function for many months to come, but it does not appear to be in any sense limiting Palestinian determination to respond to occupation. This becomes more clear when one considers the results of the stated aims of the military action.

According to Israeli army sources, 250 Palestinians have been killed, 1,500 have been arrested, and a further 3,000 have been detained for interrogation. According to an army intelligence source, 70 per cent of top wanted Palestinians have been detained or killed. By one measure, only eight of a list of 33 wanted Palestinians are still at large.

Other Israeli sources suggest a very different picture, with many of those targeted slipping away. Nor is it clear that Israeli intelligence was particularly good at identifying the most significant people. There has been little military action in Hebron, a centre of Palestinian resistance, partly because the presence of controversial Jewish settlements in the heart of the city makes military operations difficult.

Independent assessments are difficult to make, but it has to be remembered that the Israeli action was cumulative – spreading across the West Bank over more than two weeks. The earlier actions made it clear that one of the purposes was to detain or kill militia leaders, so it follows that in the later incursions there was plenty of time for key leaders to get away.

More significantly, almost all of the Hamas leadership is concentrated in Gaza, which has so far been left out of the military action. There have also been surprisingly few reports of Israeli soldiers identifying and destroying arms dumps or explosives factories, and little effort has been made to demonstrate such success. Furthermore, suicide bombings continued even during the military occupation, with devastating incidents in Haifa, Jerusalem and in the Jenin refugee camp itself.

Palestinian sources are adamant that any disruption of their paramilitary actions will be temporary at most. The *Washington Post* quoted one analyst, Samir Rantisi: 'The Israelis can capture ten activists, but the end result is there are a hundred who crop up. And those have learned the lessons of the previous ten.' As one of Sharon's advisers, Danny Ayalon, acknowledged: 'We have a few hundred that are captured members. However, we didn't touch at all the other tens of thousands, with their weapons, who are still in place.'

Finally, and most significant of all, has been the change in the status of Yassir Arafat. Far from being sidelined, his position appears to have been substantially strengthened. When one analyses this, it is quite remarkable, and almost certainly unexpected as far as Sharon's advisers are concerned.

For close to four weeks, Arafat has been restricted to a few rooms in his bombed-out headquarters, lacking electricity and sanitation facilities for most of that time. By rights, he should now be an irrelevance, yet he has become more symbolically powerful than ever before.

One key reason for this has actually been the Israeli insistence that Arafat and the Palestine Authority declare a cease-fire before a full withdrawal. But the very fact that this is required of him implies that he has such a power, and draws international attention to his position.

What next?

After four weeks of military action, any independent analysis is forced to conclude that Sharon has not increased Israel's safety or security. The evidence is actually to the contrary. Arafat is, at least for the time being, in a stronger international position than a month ago and Israel's international standing has been substantially damaged, made worse by the current opposition to the UN investigation in Jenin. Palestinian resolve appears to have been strengthened, in spite of the casualties and destruction, suicide bombings have continued, and very many young Palestinians have been further radicalised.

The Israelis have refrained, so far, from military action in Hebron, and action in Gaza has been limited. There is an international assumption that Israeli action is now more or less complete, and that a slow withdrawal will take place – the end of Sharon's Phase One. There is a further assumption that Phase Two will be some kind of enforced physical separation of the West Bank Palestinian communities.

In practice, though, the geography of Israeli settlements in the West Bank makes this formidably difficult and, in any case, Israel is so dependent on the water resources of the region that enforced separation would be against its own interests. It would, furthermore, be a tacit admission of defeat for Sharon.

More generally, one substantial effect of the recent Israeli actions has been to increase support for radical Palestinian factions, not least in Hebron but especially in Gaza. Phase Two may therefore actually be a renewed military campaign in both places. There is still little realisation outside of Israel that Sharon is single-minded in his pursuit of control and heads a government that includes even more hard-line factions and is almost entirely impervious to international opinion.

War in Hebron and Gaza may come anyway, but it will be even more likely if there are further bombs in Israeli cities.

Israel: the illusions of militarism
5 June 2002

Any independent assessment of the Israeli armed forces would initially conclude that they are remarkably strong, that they are supported by an unusually large defence expenditure, and that Israel should be able to defend itself against any likely threat. With a Jewish population of just over 5 million and a GDP of $99 billion, Israel spends about 10 per cent of its GDP on defence. Contrast this with Britain, with a population of nearly 60 million and a GDP of $1,400 billion, spending barely 2.5 per cent of its GDP on defence.

Israel's armed forces are almost as large as those of Britain, and its reserve forces are twice as large as Britain's total regular forces. It maintains nearly 4,000 tanks, compared with 600 for Britain, it has the most powerful air force in the Middle East and it is a nuclear power with at least 100 nuclear warheads that can be delivered by aircraft or by the Jericho missile.

Israel's armed forces have traditionally been geared towards rapid-manoeuvre warfare against neighbouring Arab states, with an air force capable of providing high levels of air defence combined with long-range strikes. This latter capability is being upgraded with the deployment of advanced F-15I and F-16I strike aircraft from the United States. Israel is also deploying its own anti-ballistic missile system, the Arrow, developed in close association with US aerospace companies.

In several wars with neighbouring states, Israel's armed forces have proved themselves to be both competent and effective, but not on all occasions. Operation Peace for Galilee, the invasion of Lebanon and the siege of Beirut in 1982, resulted in a huge loss of life among Palestinians and Lebanese, certainly over 10,000 people killed in a matter of months. But it also led to an occupation of much of Lebanon that was largely abandoned after three years in the face of guerrilla warfare from Hezbollah militia.

Then, as in more recent years, the Israeli army faced a war of attrition that continued in the face of its own use of massive firepower. In the first Intifada at the end of the 1980s, Israel found that many in its conscript army reacted negatively to the use of the army as a vigorous instrument of public order control in the occupied territories.

All this serves as a context for the problems that Israel now faces in maintaining its own security, problems that are more intractable than most analysts would contend. During April 2002, the Sharon government embarked on a wide-ranging offensive military operation in the West Bank. The stated purpose was to defeat the suicide bombers and to reduce Yassir Arafat to an irrelevance. But it was also apparent that a key aim was to destroy substantial parts of the infra-structure of the Palestine Authority (PA).

Much of the latter was accomplished, to the obvious displeasure of several European states that had been aiding the PA, but Arafat survived his detention and appeared to emerge with a greater standing. In addition, it is painfully obvious to the Israeli public that the military operations have singularly failed to halt the wave of suicide bombings.

Moreover, Israel has lost substantial international support outside the Middle East, especially in Europe, with much of this stemming from its operations in Nablus, Jenin and Bethlehem. In the Middle East itself, Israeli military operations have been extensively reported, not least on the satellite news channels, and this has produced a mood of bitterness directed towards Israel and its putative champion, the United States.

In the United States itself, though, support for Israel remains strong. A perception has gathered strength that the Israeli domestic experience of suicide bombings is much akin to the devastating attacks on New York and Washington last September. Furthermore, these bombings have resulted in continuing domestic support for the Sharon government, with its only possible replacement, a coalition headed by Binyamin Netanyahu, likely to be even more hard-line.

The IDF: fighting the wrong war?

In the recent military operations, it has become apparent to strategists within Israel that, for many years, the IDF have been planning for the wrong war. This may seem an extraordinary statement but it has to be appreciated that the IDF made minimal incursions into Hebron, one of the key cities of Palestinian resistance on the West Bank. They have also limited their operations into the densely packed refugee camps of Gaza to occasional forays.

The IDF experienced unusually heavy losses in the bitter fighting in Jenin, yet the refugee camp there was one of the smallest in the region. Moreover, the destruction brought about by the IDF operations caused an international outcry.

The reality is that Israel has concentrated for years on defence plans that are based on protection from external attack, whether it be from guerrilla groups in Lebanon or so-called 'second and third ring opponents' such as Iraq and particularly Iran. These plans have entailed intelligence gathering, extensive air defences, long-range strike aircraft and a highly manouevrable army. What the IDF have not done is to concentrate on urban warfare.

Again, it may seem far-fetched even to suggest that the IDF have vulnerabilities. After all, it is extraordinarily strong and well-equipped, and it has been facing poorly armed irregulars and militias in the occupied territories that are controlled by innumerable checkpoints and strategic roads. On the face of it, to talk of IDF limitations seems to be nonsense.

Perhaps so, but it is already painfully obvious that the use of massive firepower inevitably kills many people, and even the strongest forms of media control cannot prevent the images of destruction being spread across the region. It is also obvious that Palestinians remain resilient in the face of severe economic hardship, let alone deaths and injuries, and the suicide bombings continue.

The military operations in April have already displayed a wide range of limitations. The IDF face an urgent need for more helicopters and unmanned aircraft, together with all-weather, precision-guided weapons. They have relatively few troops trained in urban counter-insurgency, one of the most difficult military activities of all. The IDF are also deeply reluctant to commit ordinary infantry to such operations, especially when they are facing determined Palestinian guerrilla groups who have little to lose and may even be prepared for suicidal defensive tactics.

The IDF are perfectly capable of using overwhelming firepower against presumed centres of guerrilla activity. This was a method used repeatedly in Beirut in 1982, leading to many thousands of deaths. However, in the occupied territories, this is not possible, given the international outrage that would follow.

As a result, the IDF are urgently seeking the technologies and weapons to engage in the policy of precision strikes in dense urban environments. To put it bluntly, they do not have adequate forces for such action. Three examples illustrate their limitations. Israel has long had a policy of developing small drones for intelligence gathering. These unmanned aerial vehicles (UAVs) have been used extensively in recent weeks, but they are unarmed, unlike some of the US drones used in Afghanistan. The Israeli UAVs may identify a guerrilla group as a target, but by the time a helicopter or strike aircraft is brought in to attack it, the group has disappeared.

Another example is the type of weapon with which the helicopters are equipped. This is typically a missile designed for anti-tank warfare in open country, rather than for use in dense urban environments. The IDF also have a shortage of all-weather, precision-guided weapons, so there are many periods when they may not have the ability to attack given targets.

Israel's change of tactics

More than two months after the military operations started, it is worth reflecting that they have not been extended to the heartlands of opposition in the occupied territories. There have been brief incursions into towns and cities, such as Jenin and Nablus, in response to further suicide attacks, but Hebron and Gaza remain outside the full field of operations.

What, then, will be the approach of the Sharon government? One point to recognise is that, if there are any major incidents in Israel leading to heavy loss of life, then the IDF will be ordered into cities such as Hebron and Gaza, whatever the difficulties and international consequences.

That apart though, there are two developments currently under way. One development is to re-equip and retrain elements of the IDF to make them more effective in urban counter-insurgency. This would involve a much heavier concentration on 'remote' offensive action involving UAVs and helicopter gunships. However effective this would be, there is no doubt that future military operations will inevitably lead to many more Palestinians being killed, with the inevitable regional and wider international reactions.

The second development is an extraordinary tightening up of security throughout the occupied territories. The extent of this is only now beginning to appear in the western media, but it far exceeds most of the limitations of the past. Basically, it is a plan to encircle and isolate the eight major towns and cities of the West Bank. These include Ramallah, Jenin, Nablus, Tulkarm, Qalqilya and Hebron, and even Bethlehem, with its proximity to Jerusalem, and Jericho, down in the Jordan Valley and away from most of the areas of conflict.

According to the plan, residents of each encircled urban area will not be allowed to travel outside these areas without an IDF permit, valid for a month at a time and limited to daytime only. This will, in effect, create a permanent curfew outside the cities and towns. Furthermore, any goods entering or leaving these controlled areas will have to be unloaded on one side of a checkpoint and reloaded on to other trucks across the checkpoint. In addition, no one with Palestinian papers will be allowed into Israel itself, and this is even to include East Jerusalem, the base of many of the aid agencies working with Palestinian communities.

These stringent measures are being introduced, according to Israeli sources, to counter suicide bombings and other tactics, but they are creating a form of apartheid that Palestinians claim is every bit as repressive as the South African pass laws. Furthermore, they are likely to fundamentally damage the Palestinian economy, already in deep recession with rampant unemployment, shortages of many supplies, and 500,000 people requiring international food aid.

The Israeli economy as a target?

Israel anticipates that the combination of these severe new security measures along with changing IDF tactics will enable it to control the Palestinian Intifada. But past experience suggests the opposite. What appears much more likely is that the harsh Israeli security policies will do much to strengthen the position of the more radical Palestinian militia groups, leading to more bombings within Israel.

However much the IDF try to control the occupied territories, they cannot close them off from Israel altogether, not least because of the extensive network of Jewish settlements that stretches across the West Bank. Israeli territory therefore remains vulnerable, and more attacks will ensue, motivated by the desperation of many Palestinians.

Given the current make-up of the Israeli government, and with Netanyahu seeking his opportunity, there is little likelihood of a change of policy. Moreover, the effects of the suicide bombings are so traumatic within Israeli society that they lead to more support for the government and an even greater desire for harsher military responses. For the radical Palestinian groups, this is precisely what is intended, as they seek a greater confrontation. But for most Palestinians, it makes their predicament even worse.

In all of this there is a missing element in the analysis, the possibility that groups among the Palestinian militia may be developing a new tactic of targeting the Israeli economy rather than its people. Over the past 18 months, Palestinian paramilitary actions have involved three components: direct conflict with IDF units, attacks on settlers, and suicide attacks in Israeli cities. Rarely have there been any attempts to target the Israeli economy directly, although the impact on tourism, a significant part of the economy, has certainly been substantial, if indirect.

This may well have changed on 23 May. On that day, while most attention was focused on the aftermath of a suicide bombing at Rishon Letzion on the previous night and the Israeli killing of three Palestinian militants in Nablus, a bomb was detonated by remote control under a fuel truck parked at Israel's largest fuel depot at Herzliya near Tel Aviv. The truck was parked close to a large fuel storage tank and the bomb set fire to the truck, but the resultant blaze was extinguished before it spread to other parts of the depot.

No single group was immediately identified as responsible. The attack came shortly after Israeli security officials were said to have uncovered a plan to blow up the Azriel Towers in Tel Aviv, the tallest buildings in Israel.

Global precedents

The significance of these developments may be substantial if it indicates that Palestinian paramilitaries are starting to develop a new tactic. While this may be new as far as the Palestinian-Israeli confrontation is concerned, it is certainly not new in terms of paramilitary actions elsewhere in the world.

From 1992 to 1997, the Provisional IRA (PIRA) engaged in a series of economic targeting campaigns in Britain, including three massive bombs in London, another in Manchester, frequent and highly disruptive attacks on road and rail communications, and even attempts to disrupt electricity, gas and oil supplies.

The attacks on the central business district of London caused huge consternation at a time when London was competing with Frankfurt as the financial centre of Western Europe. While successive governments persistently denied that the PIRA campaign was a source of concern, there were many indications to the contrary, even to the extent of a much greater commitment to a peace settlement in Northern Ireland.

Many other paramilitary groups have used economic targeting and, in some cases, it has had a pronounced political effect, not least in Sri Lanka where the Tamil Tigers (LTTE) have targeted business centres, Colombo Airport, oil facilities and electricity supply lines.

What may now be starting to happen in Israel is the recognition by some Palestinian paramilitaries that such methods may be more effective in their impact on the Israeli mood than the suicide bombs in cafes, markets and bars. If this is so, then the bombing attempt on the fuel depot near Tel Aviv may prove to have a considerable long-term significance.

Moreover, if Palestinian paramilitaries seek to combine suicide bombing with the use of truck bombs, then the consequences could be extreme, as events in Sri Lanka in the mid-1990s demonstrate.

Late in 1995, the Sri Lankan army launched a massive assault on the LTTE, taking its northern stronghold of Jaffna. It was a hollow victory since the LTTE forces melted away and resorted to a devastating response in the heart of Colombo. On 31 January 1996, just seven weeks after the fall of Jaffna, a suicide bomber drove a truck packed with explosives up to the entrance to the Central Bank, in the heart of Colombo's central business district.

The massive bomb killed nearly 100 people and injured 1,400. Many key buildings were severely damaged or destroyed, including the bank itself, the Celinko Insurance building, the Colombo World Trade

Centre, the Air Lanka offices, the Bank of Ceylon, the Ceylon Hotels Corporation building and several hotels. The bombing had a considerable impact on business confidence, a problem reinforced by a further attack on the Colombo World Trade Centre two years later.

For the Israeli security authorities, their current policies of increasing control over the Palestinian population, coupled with revised military tactics, may give them the impression that they are in a position to maintain control. It is at least as likely that they may be facing quite different forms of attack.

If so, then the consequences could be extreme, confirming the belief of some security analysts that there is no alternative to a negotiated peace between Israel and the Palestinians, not least because the potential for greater violence is much more substantial than is commonly recognised.

6
Winning or Losing?

During the course of May and June 2002, the unilateral approach of the Bush administration was reinforced. Earlier policy shifts had involved withdrawal from the Kyoto Protocols on climate change and from the 1972 Anti-Ballistic Missile Treaty, together with opposition to the strengthening of the convention on biological arms control. This was now followed by opposition to some UN efforts to control the international transfers of light weapons, and by the US rescinding its signing of the charter establishing the International Criminal Court.

The world-wide war against al-Qaida and its paramilitary associates continued, but it remained difficult to bring Afghanistan under military control, substantial parts of Pakistan served as safe areas for Taliban and al-Qaida adherents, much of the leadership remained at liberty and there continued to be attacks on US and other western interests.

These included a bomb at a synagogue in Tunisia that killed 19 people, mostly German tourists, the killing of eleven French naval technicians in an attack in Karachi, another attack in the same city on the US consulate and the arrest of a group in Morocco said to be planning a series of suicide bomb attacks on the US as well as on warships in the western Mediterranean.

Thus, while the United States continued its extensive military operations, and even to commence a build-up in the Middle East for an attack on Iraq, it was difficult to conclude that it was in any real sense winning its 'war on terror'.

US unilateralism – full steam ahead?
16 May 2002

Prior to the 11 September attacks last year, there was a widespread perception in Europe that the Republican administration of George W. Bush was demonstrating a pronounced unilateralist stance on a range of international treaties and agreements. This had not been expected – indeed many commentators had taken the view that the narrowness of Bush's victory the previous November would encourage his administration to seek consensus in most areas of policy, including foreign affairs.

After 11 September a similar view was expressed in this new and troubling context. If the Bush administration was to gain widespread international support for its 'war on terror', then once again it would have to recognise the need for multilateral considerations.

Once again, expectations were not fulfilled. All the indications were that the unilateralist view remained predominant and that the United States would seek co-operation where necessary, but was fully determined to go it alone if necessary. Tensions with some sectors of the European political leadership were palpable, but there were few indications of any moderation of policy.

A consistent unilateralism?

Where are we after another four months? The war in Afghanistan continues, with the guerrilla forces becoming increasingly difficult to target; there have been further attacks including bombs killing diplomats in Islamabad, and German visitors to a synagogue in Tunis. In addition, last week's suicide bombing of the bus in Karachi killed French specialists working for the Pakistani navy on a submarine project. Powell's journeys to Israel and its neighbours failed to have a significant impact on Ariel Sharon and though the violence may have eased, it is likely to prove temporary.

Faced with these continuing foreign and security policy problems, what has been the attitude of the Bush administration? As it happens, three events in the past few days serve to throw light on the mood of the administration, but it is first worth mentioning the range of issues in which an independent or unilateral line has been taken.

Prior to George Bush's election, Republicans in Congress had opposed moves to ratify the Comprehensive Test Ban Treaty (CTBT), and voiced opposition to the continued adherence to the Anti-Ballistic Missile (ABM) Treaty and to negotiations on an anti-personnel land mine ban and an International Criminal Court.

Since its election, the US government has announced the withdrawal from the ABM Treaty, maintained opposition to the

CTBT and refused to support the protocol to strengthen the 1972 Biological and Toxin Weapons Convention. There has been a reluctance to engage in UN negotiations on the control of light arms transfers, or to participate in talks aimed at limiting weapons in space. On climate change, withdrawal from the Kyoto Protocols proposals has been accompanied by domestic measures which include a 50 per cent cut in funding for research into renewable energy sources, and a $500 million cut in the budget of the Environmental Protection Agency.

All of these examples have supported the view that the administration sees little purpose in international agreements, but is such an analysis supported by recent events?

The first indication is that last week the United States rescinded its signing of the charter for the International Criminal Court. This had been approved by Bill Clinton as one of his last acts as President, but with the known opposition of Republicans in Congress, and there was little prospect of Congress ratifying it and thereby bringing it into force for the United States. But the Bush administration has gone much further, in that it has actually reversed the decision of the previous administration, even though the establishment of the International Criminal Court has proved successful, with the 60 signatures necessary for its implementation now comfortably passed.

On the other hand, this week has seen the agreement between the United States and Russia to codify the process of cuts in strategic nuclear arsenals. This at least suggests that the US is still interested in treaties, at least those that are bilateral.

One point to make is that there is ample evidence that the current US government is prepared to maintain treaty obligations when there is no evidence that they might limit future freedom of action. This does seem to be the case in this US-Russian agreement. But it is a treaty that is radically different from the SALT (Strategic Arms Limitation Treaty), START (Strategic Arms Reduction Treaty) and INF (Intermediate Nuclear Forces) treaties of the Cold War era, which had considerable detail embodied in them with clearly defined verification provisions.

There might yet be such provisions in the new agreement, but it is clear that it does not place any limits on existing US plans for its nuclear forces. A substantial proportion of the warheads that are withdrawn will simply be put into storage and can be returned to service later. There are no limits on the modernising of existing systems, nor are there limits on developing and building new types of warheads.

In short, the US-Russian agreement does make official some of the cuts that are already taking place, and this is certainly to be welcomed. At the same time, it gives an impression of progress. But put alongside the recent US Nuclear Posture Review, it allows unrestricted development of all the programmes that are now being investigated.

A widening axis

Perhaps the clearest indication of a forceful security policy came from a recent lecture to the Heritage Foundation by John Bolton of the State Department, a notably hard-line member of the inner security circle in Washington.

Bolton was absolutely clear in making the connection between terrorism and those unacceptable states believed to be developing weapons of mass destruction. To put it bluntly, they will not be allowed to do so:

> States that sponsor terror and pursue WMD [weapons of mass destruction] must stop. States that renounce terror and abandon WMD can become part of our effort. But those that do not can expect to become our targets.

Bolton went on to extend the 'axis of evil' to three additional states defined by him to be 'sponsors of terrorism that are pursuing or that have the potential to pursue weapons of mass destruction or have the capability to do so in violation of their treaty obligations'.

Bolton cited Syria and Libya in this category, with strong comments on each. But the surprise came in the inclusion of Cuba, partly on the basis that Cuba has an advanced biomedical industry and supplies pharmaceuticals and vaccines to countries throughout the south. It therefore has the capability to spread dual-use technologies that could aid the development of biological weapons, and Bolton cited unnamed analysts and Cuban defectors who are suspicious of the Cuban biomedical industry.

The speech caused concern in many quarters, and his comments on Cuba were partially eclipsed by Jimmy Carter's subsequent visit. At the same time, the message was clear – the axis of evil is not restricted to Iraq, Iran and North Korea; it is in the process of being extended and Cuba is now a part of it.

In overall terms, the mood within the Bush administration remains forcefully in the direction of a long-lasting war on terror. Iraq may remain the key state, but others are beginning to come into the picture, the clear surprise being Cuba.

An arc of conflict
23 May 2002

Events a month or so ago demonstrated that guerrilla forces in Afghanistan, whether Taliban, al-Qaida or others, were largely operating in very small groups and were able to hide out in Afghan villages and towns. They were also able to disperse over the border in Pakistan, and were showing a surprising adaptability to US military tactics.

Other points were evident. They included the increase in numbers of western forces engaged in Afghanistan and the reluctance of the Pakistani government to allow a heavy US presence in the region bordering Afghanistan. There was also the prospect of the spring thaw opening up mountain passes for guerrilla movements, as well as the longer-term effects of the Israeli-Palestinian confrontation as a radicalising factor in the wider region.

It was also pointed out that while there had been no recent deaths among western forces, there was evidence of quite frequent attacks on units of these forces. The key point here was that the guerrillas were still capable of military initiative, a further indication that to talk of 'mopping up' operations was, at the very least, premature.

Over the past two weeks there have been a number of developments. Even when put together they do not give us a completely reliable indication of likely trends, but they do help to illuminate what is happening.

A phantom enemy

At the level of military operations, western forces have still found it repeatedly difficult to target active guerrilla groups. Time and again, troops have failed to make contact, and even the much-vaunted destruction of a large arms dump was questioned when there were indications that it was not part of a Taliban or al-Qaida supply system.

The British Marines have been involved in three operations, Ptarmigan, Snipe and Condor, the last-named being last week's move to support an Australian Special Forces unit that had apparently come under guerrilla attack. In the event, none of the three operations involved direct contact with guerrilla forces.

Even so, attacks on coalition forces have continued, including the death of a member of the US Special Forces. There has also been a steady increase in the western military presence in Afghanistan. The International Security Assistance Force, centred almost entirely on Kabul, remains at about 5,000 troops, and this is engaged essentially in local security.

There are quite separate forces engaged in offensive operations elsewhere in the country, and these now number around 11,000. While the largest group is from the United States (5,000), there are sizeable contingents from Canada (2,200), and Britain (1,700). Several other western countries are also involved, notably France and Germany.

Sources in Pakistan suggest that there are currently only a few hundred guerrilla fighters active, with the great majority having dispersed into villages and towns, and especially into some of the larger cities in Pakistan. Even so, these active fighters are able to ensure that a substantial western military presence remains in Afghanistan, with this directed much more at counter-guerrilla actions than in aiding Afghanistan in nation-building and reconstruction.

UN sources have repeatedly called for a much larger security assistance force, perhaps around 30,000 instead of the current 5,000, in order to ensure reasonable levels of security across the country. At present, though, coalition states are reluctant to accept this and, under US leadership, persist with an offensive military strategy.

The reluctance of Pakistan

Within Pakistan, militant anti-western groups remain active, as evidenced by the attack on the French naval workers two weeks ago. But the Pakistan government is increasingly resistant to allowing US Special Forces freedom of operations within its territory. There are two reasons for this. One is the obvious risk of a further rise in the current anti-American mood, with the probability that this becomes more directed towards the government itself.

The other is the huge preoccupation of the Pakistani military with the current dangerous confrontation with India. Pakistan simply does not have the military forces to confront India while, at the same time, co-operating with the United States in counter-guerrilla operations in the border region. But without those forces, it is unwilling to let the United States operate on its own, at least not in terms of engaging in serious open conflict on its territory.

A further problem for Pakistan is that its own armed forces are relatively poorly equipped, not least because of the effect of sanctions. As a result, Pakistan is pressing the United States for upgrades to its F-16 fleet, and the release of spare parts embargoed since the nuclear tests in 1998. The US may accede to these requests in return for greater freedom of action in Pakistan itself, but Pakistan's view is that it has already done more than enough to support the US.

All this means that the ability of the US and its coalition partners to engage in operations in Pakistan remains very limited. Meanwhile, al-Qaida and Taliban guerrillas can simply bide their time while undertaking sufficient attacks on coalition forces to keep them heavily engaged in Afghanistan for a long time to come.

The US homeland under threat?

The remarkable sequence of events in the United States in the past two weeks leads us to ask one key question – is there really a possibility of a further major al-Qaida attack? There is no doubt that President Bush has come under some pressure because of revelations about warnings given prior to 11 September. But it is not a serious blow to his credibility and domestic opinion remains supportive of his 'war on terror'. Why, then, be so upfront about new threats unless there really is a risk?

Two explanations can be offered for such talk. One is simply that there is some small possibility of another attack and the administration wants to be absolutely sure that it cannot be accused of not disseminating a warning in advance. In a sense, this is all about routine politics, but it may also disguise the issue of the actual status of al-Qaida.

In that context, there are several points to make. One is that, as has been mentioned, guerrilla forces remain active in the region, and are tying down over 10,000 coalition troops. The second is that the disruption of the al-Qaida leadership has been very limited – few have been killed or captured.

Then there is the pretty obvious fact that the Taliban and al-Qaida prisoners at Camp X-Ray and in Afghanistan have failed to yield much serious intelligence about either organisation. Finally, anti-American feeling in the Middle East and South-west Asia remains high, making it easier for al-Qaida and other groups to operate, gain finance and move around.

There are two other elements to consider. One is that the very dispersal of al-Qaida from Afghanistan may be to its advantage. A concentration in one country, even under the sympathetic control of the Taliban, may have offered protection, but it is actually more difficult for western intelligence and security agencies to track operatives across numerous countries, especially when there is so much support for their activities.

The other element, always to be remembered, is that the al-Qaida network is part of a regional phenomenon with very clear political aims (US military out of the Gulf and the fall of the House of Saud), and that these aims form part of a long-term strategy.

Within that strategy, the New York and Washington massacres were specifically designed, in part, to increase US engagement across the region, with the anticipated effect that this would engender a stronger regional reaction. We can assume that this strategy is still in place and, as such, a further major attack would form an integral part of it.

Iran in the line of fire

The other significant development of the past week is the manner in which forceful warnings have been issued from the Bush administration about terrorist use of weapons of mass destruction. There is certainly some possibility that a paramilitary group could acquire and use such weapons, but the warnings seem more directed at serving a political purpose – that of preparing the ground for an attack on Iraq.

In this context, the connection is being made repeatedly between terrorism and 'rogue' states that seek weapons of mass destruction, with Iran labelled as the main problem. This has been to the evident surprise of many European politicians who have been steadfastly cultivating good relations with the current government in Tehran, widely seen in Western Europe as relatively moderate in outlook.

Part of the reason for the US focus on Iran must be the historic problem of memories of the hostage crisis going right back to the late 1970s. It is worth remembering, though, that the one country that has consistently regarded Iran as the major regional threat has been Israel, and current US attitudes to Iran are almost certainly hardened by the currently strong pro-Israel sentiment in Washington.

The Israeli view is that Iran, in concert with Syria, is deeply involved in anti-Israeli action, not just through arms shipments to the Palestinians, but in its support for Hezbollah in southern Lebanon. This view now has substantial credence in Washington, yet European governments are far more concerned to seek co-operation rather than confrontation with Tehran. At the very least, this will be a source of friction in Euro-American relations.

Iraq: a moving target

The status of Iran, as the newly confirmed 'lead rogue state', does not diminish the concern with Iraq, not least because of a near-unanimous belief in Washington that Iraq is much closer to having weapons of mass destruction, especially biological weapons, and that this is simply unacceptable.

One problem, though, is that the Saddam Hussein regime itself appears resilient and stable, and is experiencing more favourable economic circumstances than for many years. The last two or three years have seen a significant improvement, per capita GDP growing by 15 per cent last year. Moreover, this is not just affecting the elite of around 1 million people who have done well throughout the past decade, but even the poorer sectors of Iraqi society are experiencing some benefit, in contrast to extreme difficulties over many years.

Smuggling of oil exports persists at a high level, but Iraq has also exercised more open pragmatism in seeking much closer diplomatic and economic relations with neighbouring states. According to the *Washington Post*, Iraq is importing $13 billion worth of goods from neighbours such as Turkey, Egypt, Syria, Jordan and even Saudi

Arabia, and a sustained diplomatic process has eased relations with many Middle Eastern countries.

The Saddam Hussein regime remains firmly in power, and brutal and repressive measures continue to be used. But some neighbouring states now see a degree of pragmatism and caution that makes them less fearful of the regime. This combines with the regional attitudes to Israel and the United States to create a mood that is resistant to any further western intervention in Iraq.

It is in marked contrast to the mood in Washington, where the Iraqi regime remains the focus of attention, with every sign of military action later this year or early next year. At the very least, and from a regional perspective, Iraq's recent economic advance makes that much more problematic.

The limits of military power
29 May 2002

In the past few days, there have been two surprising demonstrations of the limits of military power. The US Joint Chiefs of Staff have warned the Bush administration against rushing into an attack on Iraq and the Israelis have conspicuously failed in their use of harsh military measures to control the suicide bombings. In the first of two articles, the implications of the changing US military attitude to Iraq are explored. Next week's article (see page 131) will analyse the problems facing the Israeli Defence Forces as they confront bitter opposition in the densely populated towns and refugee camps of the West Bank and Gaza.

Iraq: military caution

An underlying feature of the US 'war on terror' has been a sustained commitment to overthrowing the Saddam Hussein regime in Iraq. There have been many attempts to link the regime to terrorist activities elsewhere in the world, with virtually no success. Yet President Bush's labelling of Iraq as one part of the 'axis of evil' was a clear indication of the deep opposition to the regime. The reasons for this are clear, and comprise two elements.

One, very obviously, is that it is unacceptable to US foreign policy to have such a regime in the heart of the world's most strategically important oil-bearing region. Iraq alone has about 11 per cent of the world's oil reserves – about four times as much as the United States (including Alaska) – and it is in the middle of a region with almost two-thirds of the world total, at least ten times as great as the much-vaunted Caspian Basin reserves. In Washington's view, to have an oppositional and possibly expansionist regime right in the middle of such a region is a continuing and wholly unacceptable security risk.

Even more important than this, though, is the recognition that one of the key components of the regime's security posture is to develop its own deterrent forces, principally comprising chemical and biological weapons and delivery systems. For four years it has escaped UN inspections; there is an assumption that it is working vigorously to weaponise its CBW (chemical and biological weapons) systems; and there is a belief that this will serve as a powerful limitation on any intervention, exactly as the Iraqi regime intends it to do.

For the United States, this is utterly unacceptable. It is simply inconceivable to have a situation where a rogue state could deter the United States and its allies from taking action in pursuit of their own security interests. There are bitter memories of the ability of the Iraqis to develop biological weapons in the run-up to the 1991 Gulf War and of the limitations that this placed on coalition action.

Mainly for these reasons, the termination of the Iraqi regime is regarded as a necessity in Washington, and there have been numerous indications that a major military operation would be initiated later this year with the aim of destroying the regime.

Now come credible reports that the US Joint Chiefs of Staff, having done detailed assessments of the needs and nature of such an operation, are urging caution. At the very least they say that a war with Iraq would be fraught with difficulty, and that substantial time would be needed to develop the forces. There are even indications that alternatives might be sought, perhaps through the use of Special Forces or by encouraging internal opposition to the regime and thereby fostering rebellion and collapse.

The logic of restraint

At first sight, this seems an extraordinary situation. By almost universal consent, the United States is the world's pre-eminent power, with military forces of extraordinary capability, able to take action in any part of the world and backed up by incredibly powerful tactical and strategic nuclear forces. There is a dedicated military command, Central Command (CENTCOM), concerned exclusively with the region, the Fifth Fleet patrols the Persian Gulf, and one side-effect of the Afghanistan War has been the development of bases across South-west and Central Asia.

Furthermore, the Iraqi armed forces are far weaker than they were at the time of the Gulf War, with the army only half its previous strength and the air force practically non-existent. Two no-fly zones have pinned down Iraqi forces and limited their operations, and the whole country has been under punitive sanctions for more than a decade. In such circumstances, a determined effort to destroy the regime should be very much more straightforward than eleven years ago.

This is not how the Joint Chiefs see it, with a stated requirement of at least 200,000 troops and the risk of substantial casualties. So what are the factors that account for this unexpected caution?

There are many explanations, but three are particularly important. The first is that the United States does not have the regional support that was forthcoming in 1991. Then, Kuwait had been occupied, Saudi Arabia was apparently threatened and Iraq was seen as a regional threat. Although the great majority of the coalition forces were American, there were substantial numbers from Britain and France, Arab countries such as Egypt and Syria contributed significant numbers of ground troops, and more than 25 other countries participated.

This time, the United States is far more isolated. There is some support from Britain, although the government is far more cautious in private than it admits in public. Other European countries are highly dubious, and support in the Middle East is absent apart from some smaller Gulf states, and even they are urging caution.

The second factor is that this lack of regional support hugely limits any military operation, especially in relation to launch-points for an invasion of Iraq. In 1991, the Saudi authorities allowed coalition forces almost uninterrupted access to their territory, as well as committing their own forces. Turkey, too, was available for military operations.

Now, there is doubt over whether the Saudis would even allow US aircraft to operate from their bases, and little if any chance of troops being allowed to invade Iraq across the Saudi border. This leaves the much smaller territory of Kuwait as the only launch-point. Turkey might allow the basing of offensive air forces, but full-scale US troop movements would be highly unlikely. Other neighbours of Iraq, notably Iran and Syria, are hardly going to be supportive – not when they have been designated part of the 'axis of evil', and when their own domestic public opinion is so vigorously anti-American.

Finally, the Iraqi regime itself appears to be firmly in control aided by the recent economic upturn which has allowed, among other things, an increase in military spending. It is true that the regime does not have the military power of eleven years ago, and there is certainly the strong possibility that elements of the armed forces might turn on the regime if faced with an all-out US invasion. But this is by no means certain.

The core units of the Iraqi army, the Republican Guard and Special Republican Guard, together with large elements of the security apparatus, have much to lose if the regime falls, and their loyalty may therefore remain strong in the face of an invasion. Furthermore, while most Iraqis have experienced all the consequences of a brutal regime, coupled with more than a decade of sanctions, much of the blame for this is laid at the door of the United States, not the regime.

The consequence is that any attempt to destroy the regime, especially if it involves an occupation of Baghdad, could lead to intense urban warfare with many Americans killed. Furthermore, regime survival is at the heart of Saddam Hussein's strategy. It has to be assumed that an attempt to destroy the regime itself – which is, after all, the intended aim of the whole operation – will most likely lead to the Iraqis using any chemical and biological weapons that they may now have. Moreover, such weapons would be used not just against US troops in Iraq itself, but against targets in neighbouring countries such as Kuwait.

In extreme circumstances of imminent regime destruction, attacks against Israel might even be contemplated in the expectation that there would be a massive response from the Sharon government leading to regional escalation. Given the existing levels of anti-American feeling across the Middle East, greatly exacerbated by recent Israeli actions, even an attack on Iraq that did not bring in Israel would heighten tensions to a remarkable degree.

The Afghanistan connection

Even with these substantial problems and limitations, there still has to be a question mark over why the US Joint Chiefs have taken this cautious view. After all, Iraq is not a strong state and US forces are formidable. Furthermore, if Iraq is left alone, its further development of weapons of mass destruction in such a strategically important region would surely be a nightmare for the Bush administration, with its need to regain international control after 11 September. To have the world's leading rogue state able to act with impunity could not be tolerated.

Are there other reasons for the caution? The answer is yes, and they stem from some of the less obvious features of the military actions of the past eight months. As has been argued throughout this series of articles, the 'war on terror' has been much less easy to fight than most elements of the media would have us believe. Where there have been direct confrontations between US troops and guerrilla forces, the latter have fought with a remarkable determination. The United States has suffered casualties and much equipment damage and has ended up leading a coalition of some 11,000 troops in Afghanistan itself, with tens of thousands deployed regionally.

In the past three months the guerrilla forces have almost entirely gone to ground; they have proved extraordinarily difficult to intercept. Most are hidden in cities, towns and villages in Pakistan. That country, hugely preoccupied with Kashmir and the risk of an appalling confrontation with India, is deeply reluctant to give the United States a free hand in the border areas, and cannot spare the troops to confront the guerrillas itself.

More generally, the pace of military operations in the region as a whole has put a strain on many of the US units. There has been a substantial increase in accidents involving aircraft, large numbers have had to be withdrawn from service for maintenance and repairs, and the whole system is experiencing some quite serious strain. Furthermore, the rate at which missiles and precision-guided bombs have been used has resulted in serious shortages. It will take many months to restore the stocks, let alone to build them up to the levels required for an all-out assault on Iraq.

Meanwhile, there is no guarantee whatsoever that the war in Afghanistan is over – indeed there are recent indications of a reforming of some Taliban elements, with the bitter rivalries between warlords giving them an opportunity to regain influence. While the Taliban is almost universally discredited outside of Afghanistan, it is worth remembering that it came to power in the mid-1990s precisely because it brought some sort of order, however harsh, to an anarchic country crippled by warlordism.

What next for Iraq?

If the US is limited in its immediate ability to attack the Saddam Hussein regime, one major alternative might be to combine support for oppositional forces with more intensive air attacks and the use of Special Forces, progressively crippling the regime and ensuring its collapse.

It sounds possible in theory, but there are three immediate problems. Oppositional groups are fractured and weak, sustained air attacks with their inevitable civilian casualties would strengthen opposition to US actions in the region and in Europe, and US Special Forces are already under heavy pressure because of operations in Afghanistan, Georgia, the Philippines and elsewhere. In short, there is a discontinuity between what the Bush administration believes is essential, destroying the Iraqi regime, and the capabilities of the US military to do it.

This all goes a long way to explaining why President Bush was so careful to emphasise the need for co-operation with European partners during his meetings in Germany last week. It may also explain his considerable efforts to support President Putin in Moscow, as Russian opposition to a war on Iraq would certainly be a limitation. What this all means is that, at least in the context of Iraq, the Bush administration is recognising the limitations on 'going it alone', so more protracted efforts may be made to bring the Europeans on board.

At the same time, we should not be under any illusion that the administration is in any way downgrading its determination to terminate the Saddam Hussein regime. That remains a fundamental requirement, not least to demonstrate that oppositional states must simply not be allowed to develop weapons of mass destruction. The security advisers close to Bush will maintain their stance, and there may well be questions over why the Joint Chiefs of Staff are so cautious at a time of burgeoning defence budgets.

Even so, what these potential limits to US military power do indicate is that European allies may be more important than anyone realised. With that comes the potential to exert some influence on Washington in its policies towards the Middle East. More generally, the military caution over attacking Iraq might just be the first sign that the strongly unilateralist tendencies of the Bush administration are starting to hit some limits.

The al-Qaida threat remains
19 June 2002

The political assembly of Afghan leaders in Kabul, the Loya Jirga, has made some progress, and Hamid Karzai is established as the political leader of Afghanistan until elections are held in two years' time. Even so, there have been numerous controversies over the role of a number of warlords in their attempts to control parts of the country. It is also clear that there is considerable opposition in many of the Pashtun parts of the country to what is perceived to be a concentration of political power in the hands of Tajik and Uzbek groups in the north.

At the same time, there has been less disruption to the negotiations than some had anticipated, and Kabul itself is reasonably peaceful, even if the same is not true for much of the country. There is still no sign of the extension of the International Security Assistance Force (ISAF) to the rest of the country. This is regarded as a prerequisite for ensuring stability during state-building, but ISAF remains restricted to about 5,000 troops in and around the capital, instead of the 30,000 or more recommended by UN officials and others.

There is, to put it bluntly, no political will in coalition countries to assemble such a force, and this calls into question the longer-term prospects for Afghanistan to attain a degree of normality. Moreover, there have already been considerable problems in aiding the development of a national army for Afghanistan.

Meanwhile, combat operations by British, US and other troops against Taliban guerrillas in eastern Afghanistan have yielded little except for the occasional destruction of arms dumps. The Taliban have gone to ground, both in Afghanistan and Pakistan, and al-Qaida operatives have dispersed, not just into Pakistan but across the whole region.

Al-Qaida: dispersed, but active

In May, there were indications that the US government was anticipating a further paramilitary attack, and there was much speculation about the status of al-Qaida and its capability for further action. Events over the past ten days have thrown some light on this, and these suggest that the organisation is indeed active and has already had some involvement in a number of attacks.

The 'dirty bomb' story that attracted so much attention last week is certainly not the most significant indicator. Initially, the story was hyped up to a remarkable degree, with suggestions that a radiological bomb attack on Washington was in an advanced state of development.

Later, it became apparent that the man arrested, Jose Padilla, was at best a small-time associate of al-Qaida. He had originally gone to them with unworkable plans for an H-bomb that he had obtained from an Internet site. But he was told to 'think small' and sent back to the US to do reconnaissance for the possible development of a radiological bomb.

That al-Qaida should be considering such a weapon is no surprise, although most analysts believe that further attacks will use more conventional methods. But it is some of the other developments that are more important.

When put together, the attacks and attempted actions of the past few months all indicate that al-Qaida is active, if more dispersed than last autumn. Among the incidents were the attack on a church in the heavily defended diplomatic compound in Islamabad earlier this year, and the bombing last month of a bus in Karachi carrying technicians to work at a Pakistani naval project supported by France. This bomb was the result of careful planning; it was a substantial explosion and it killed eleven French engineers and three other people.

Earlier, on 11 April, an attack on a synagogue in Tunisia killed five Tunisians and 14 German tourists. Though initially thought to be accidental, it was later established as intentional and evidence has emerged of a link with al-Qaida.

In the past ten days, there have been two major incidents. One was the attack on the US consulate in Karachi. The other was the arrest of three Saudi citizens in Morocco believed to have been planning a series of suicide bomb attacks against western warships in the western Mediterranean.

The attack on the US consulate was a huge explosion, inflicting substantial damage on what was actually a heavily fortified building reinforced specifically against such an attack. It killed eleven people and injured 26. It has resulted in the withdrawal of almost all US diplomatic staff from Pakistan and has caused the US State Department to reconsider its staffing policies in missions right across the region.

The group planning to attack warships from Morocco was also involved in careful and long-term planning and, if it had succeeded in pressing home an attack against an aircraft carrier or an amphibious warfare ship, could have killed scores if not hundreds of people.

What is al-Qaida's strategy?

Not all of these incidents may have been directly planned by al-Qaida, but they do indicate an active organisation that is continuing with a long-term strategy. This stretches back at least ten years and is probably intended to go on for at least as long, the principal aim being the end of what is perceived as a US military occupation in the Persian Gulf and Saudi Arabia, and the fall of the House of Saud.

Over the past ten years, there has been a series of major attacks against the United States, beginning with the attempt to destroy the World Trade Center in 1993. They continued with the Khobar Towers barracks bomb at Dhahran in 1996, individual attacks on US service personnel in Saudi Arabia, the East African embassy bombings of 1998 and, more recently, the attack on the USS *Cole* in Aden harbour.

The key questions are how this all relates to the al-Qaida network and what it tells us about its future capabilities. On the first point, it is almost certainly a mistake to see al-Qaida as a strictly hierarchical and integrated organisation. If this were so, the problem for US and other security forces would be relatively straightforward.

In practice, it is more sensible to view al-Qaida as part of a rather loose series of organisations with many cross-connections and a general consensus about the nature of the 'enemy' (the United States in particular), and who share training, logistics and financial support.

It is also the case that the great majority of the al-Qaida personnel have not been captured or killed in Afghanistan – indeed many of them left the country some months ago. It does seem likely that al-Qaida underestimated the way in which the US would use the Northern Alliance as its proxy ground forces, and the network probably expected that it would have safe locations in Afghanistan through the winter.

While this would have disrupted the organisation, it has certainly not destroyed its capacity to act. Indeed, there are reliable indications that the leadership has dispersed operational authority to a number of middle-ranking members of the organisation who may be operating, at least to an extent, independently of each other.

Much of the recent information about the status of al-Qaida has come as a result of the Moroccan interrogation of the Saudis detained for the plan to bomb warships, but it is worth noting that Morocco is almost certainly collaborating more closely with the CIA than any other Arab country. As a consequence, it would be wise to assume that other al-Qaida groups may be planning actions elsewhere with less difficulty.

The one thing to remember about the group is that it is planning for the long term. While the full details of the planning of the 11 September attacks are not yet clear, it is apparent that the operation had been under development for a long time. It should also be assumed that other operations are at an earlier stage of development, and may have been started well before last September.

More generally, we also have to recognise that one of the core aims of last September's atrocities was to incite the United States to a broadly based military response in South-west Asia, with the aim of inciting greater anti-American sentiments.

This aim has been much aided by the plight of the Palestinians. Even though al-Qaida has shown little interest in the Israeli-Palestinian confrontation in the past, it is certainly gaining by the widespread perception throughout the region that the United States is behind Sharon and against the Palestinians. Whatever the validity of this perception, it is solidly held in the Middle East and aids al-Qaida in getting financial and other support for its strategy.

Perhaps the key thing to remember is that the two events last week, the Karachi bomb and the Moroccan plan to bomb warships, indicate an organisation that is very far from being in its final throes. Indeed, the very fact that it is much more dispersed outside Afghanistan probably makes it more difficult to track and intercept. In the short term, the disruption of its Afghanistan base may have limited al-Qaida's potential for further action. In the long term, it may have aided it.

Al-Qaida: the weapon of patience
26 June 2002

In examining the status and capabilities of al-Qaida in last week's article, one conclusion was that the organisation clearly remains active, with a number of recent incidents demonstrating its capability for paramilitary attacks across the world. It also seems likely that al-Qaida is operating in a dispersed mode, with many planning decisions left to middle-level activists. Both of these aspects have been demonstrated by incidents reported in the past week, with emphasis shifting from Pakistan, Morocco and the United States to Saudi Arabia.

Thirteen suspected members of al-Qaida have been detained by the Saudi authorities on suspicion of smuggling weapons and explosives into the country in preparation for paramilitary actions. There is a suspicion that the action may be connected with an attempt to shoot down a US warplane taking off from a heavily protected air base in a remote part of the kingdom. Of those arrested, eleven are Saudis, one is Sudanese and one is from Iraq.

The Sudanese man is reported to have been responsible for the anti-aircraft attack, having been able to get the missile in from Yemen, with local assistance. He is believed to have escaped to Sudan, only to be extradited to Saudi Arabia following interrogation.

Behind Saudi lines

It is hardly surprising that al-Qaida is active in Saudi Arabia, given the strong thread of support for the organisation in the kingdom. Furthermore, since the organisation is specifically seeking the overthrow of the Saudi royal family, and the country has been the site of a number of attacks in recent years, it should be expected that the Saudi authorities will react with considerable determination.

The attack on the US plane is one of several recent incidents in the kingdom, including a sniper attack on an Australian employee of BAE Systems working in the north of the country. There have, separately, been a number of car bombings affecting expatriates, including the murder of a British banker last week. The Saudi authorities have said that these latter incidents stem from criminal activities involving illicit alcohol, but their insistence on this explanation is not hugely convincing.

In any case, what is now clear is that the aircraft attack has some more general implications and was more serious than earlier press reports indicated. According to a well-informed US journal, *Aviation Week*, the attacker fired a shoulder-launched SA-7 anti-aircraft missile at a plane and then panicked, burying a second missile before escaping.

On one level, the attack may be a relatively minor worry for the Pentagon. The SA-7 is an early Soviet surface-to-air missile, now manufactured in several other countries including China and Pakistan. It requires considerable training and experience to work effectively, and it is quite easy to avoid with counter-measures. Its threat hardly compares with the American Stinger missile used to some effect by US-backed forces in Afghanistan in the 1980s.

This, though, is not the point. What is significant is that groups in Saudi Arabia are able to import and use SA-7 missiles and to do so against this particular air base, one of the most securely guarded US Air Force locations in the world. Back in 1996, the US air base near Dhahran was the target for a truck bomb that killed 19 Americans and injured 500 people. A sewage truck loaded with explosives was parked and detonated in front of a high-rise barracks block, the Khobar Towers, collapsing the whole of the front of the building.

At the time, the Dhahran base was the key air base for US forces in Saudi Arabia, but it was close to the city and regarded as insecure in the face of such threats. As a result, a new base was built, out in the desert, and at a cost of around $500 million. This is the Prince Sultan Air Base, the main command and control centre for the US Air Force in the region, housing some 4,000 US service personnel.

The base has an intense perimeter security system, and a tenth of its entire personnel are involved solely in this activity. It is not a happy base, in that there are severe restrictions on people serving there in terms of movements away from the base. Though they may be very secure while there, they are also, to an extent, prisoners of an insecure environment.

The air force believes that the base is virtually immune to attack, even by suicide bombers. This may be so, but it is clear that it is possible for determined paramilitaries to get within range of low-flying planes and attempt to shoot them down. In a sense, the SA-7 attack was symbolic – it showed that Saudi Arabia has to be considered as something akin to a war zone for US military forces, even though one of the prime aims of US policy in the region is to support the current Saudi regime.

The SA-7 attack was unlikely to work, but more advanced missiles such as the SA-16 and SA-18 may become available to paramilitaries in due course, giving the US Air Force much greater concern.

Afghanistan and the Philippines: US forces remain

Meanwhile, in Afghanistan, the UK Marines contingent is due to depart shortly, having completed a range of high altitude operations designed to counter guerrilla activity. Apart from two arms caches, one of which may not have had anything to do with guerrilla forces, the Marines have had virtually no contact with Taliban or al-Qaida units. Their actions may have prevented a certain regrouping of the forces, but it seems more likely that they have merged back into communities on both sides of the Afghanistan–Pakistan border.

Among the arms found by coalition forces operating in eastern Afghanistan in the first two weeks of June were 30 Chinese-made SA-7 missiles of the kind fired in Saudi Arabia.

Although Britain may be withdrawing most of its forces, the US view is that their own troops will stay in Afghanistan for at least another year. The US currently has about 7,000 troops in the country, about 3,000 each at two major bases – Bagram and Kandahar – and others operating in small units, mostly in the east of Afghanistan close to the Pakistan border. US military commanders characterise it as a counter-insurgency operation, mostly against numerous small guerrilla groups, but with up to 1,000 concentrated close to the border.

One US commander has stated that not all of the guerrilla forces are ideological, saying that many 'tend to be criminal (rather) than anything nationalistic and idealistic', but did accept that they could be sustained, in part, by sympathetic local people.

While the US presence in Afghanistan is set to continue, the Special Forces missions in the Philippines were due to be completed by the end of July. This now looks unlikely and the prospect is actually for an increased commitment to counter-insurgency training there. This turnround follows a recent visit to Basilan Island by Paul Wolfowitz, Donald Rumsfeld's deputy at the Pentagon.

While the Abu Sayyaf guerrilla group has recently experienced reversals, it remains active, and a joint patrol of US Marines and Philippine army units came under fire for the first time on 18 June.

Al-Qaida's future

There has been some surprise by security analysts that the al-Qaida network has not staged another major attack on the United States, given that it is clearly active in a number of countries and almost certainly has the capability to mount a substantial paramilitary operation.

It is possible that this is due to the much increased levels of security in the United States, the degree of intelligence co-operation between the US and some of its allies, and the possible effects of the disruption to the al-Qaida network caused by the war in Afghanistan.

This may all be true, but it does not fit in with al-Qaida's ability to mount attacks in Pakistan and Tunisia, its evident activity in Morocco and Saudi Arabia, and repeated warnings by US officials about further attacks.

There is a quite different explanation, which is much less appealing to western officials but may be more accurate. Put simply, al-Qaida does not need to stage any more attacks at present because the United States is doing an effective public relations job on its behalf.

The reasoning behind this is clear-cut. The long-term aim of the network is to develop a sustained movement based on radical Islamic ideas but politically directed against the United States and its allies, especially states such as Saudi Arabia in the Middle East.

Such a movement is enhanced if al-Qaida can show itself to be a significant force able to have a severe effect on the United States, and if the US itself persists with policies in the Middle East that tend to encourage anti-American radicalism.

From al-Qaida's point of view, the Bush administration is currently performing both of these functions with admirable skill and commitment. Thus, it is delivering frequent warnings about the danger of further terrorist attacks, the 'dirty bomb' story being a very good example. Such warnings are reported around the world, and give the impression that al-Qaida is highly active and can even be said to have the US 'on the run'. This may not be the case, but it is the impression that counts, especially in the Middle East.

Furthermore, both of Bush's main policy planks in the Middle East play to al-Qaida's support in the region. While an attack on Iraq may not happen for many months, the very idea of the US gearing up for military action is a strong reminder of its determination to keep the Gulf secure for what are perceived to be its own narrow interests.

Even more useful to al-Qaida is the Bush stance on the Israeli-Palestinian confrontation, with this week's policy speech making it absolutely clear that Israel's war against the Palestinians is seen as part of the world-wide war on terror.

It is probably the case that al-Qaida currently has the capability for another major attack, and it could happen at any time. Even so, from the al-Qaida perspective, it may not be necessary in relation to its long-term aims. At some stage a further attack could happen but, for now, the policies of the Bush administration may actually be making it unnecessary.

7
Endless War

During the latter part of 2002, there was a belief in Washington that a robust attitude to ensuring the security of the Middle East was the best policy for the United States. This involved firm support for Israel, a good working relationship with acceptable elite regimes in the region, the termination of the Saddam Hussein regime in Iraq and the successful countering of paramilitary groups wherever they threatened US interests.

Robust security was now certainly seen to extend to pre-emptive action, with this including the targeting and killing of paramilitary suspects in countries such as Lebanon, together with the extensive detention of many hundreds of people at Camp X-Ray pending possible eventual trials before military tribunals.

As the United States pursued its security concerns, there was little recognition that the 'majority world' continued to see these developments in a very different light, going far beyond a legitimate war on paramilitary violence to constitute an attempt to dominate global affairs. Moreover, much of the concern felt across Latin America, Africa and much of Asia was also being shared by many European states, especially in relation to US policy in the Middle East.

Perhaps most surprising was the persistence of the view in the United States that its 'war on terror' was succeeding. This contrasted with the situation in Afghanistan, where at least 10,000 US troops were engaged in an ongoing guerrilla conflict, and also with the continued activity of al-Qaida and its affiliates with attacks such as those in Bali and Kenya.

Furthermore, the increasingly direct involvement of the United States in the Horn of Africa, the Persian Gulf and Central Asia were all leading to a deepening resentment, not least in the Arab world, over what was very widely seen as foreign control of substantial regions. In particular this was seen to be in pursuit of its own economic interests, especially increasing the control of the immense oil reserves of the Persian Gulf as well as those of the Caspian Basin.

What was most relevant here, but still unrecognised within the Bush administration, was the risk that such a security posture was a persistent advantage to organisations such as al-Qaida, helping to ensure their continuing support and thus making it likely that paramilitary responses against the United States would ultimately get worse.

From deterrence to pre-emption?
The US military after 9/11
3 July 2002

A full account of the tragic events in the village of Kakarak in the Oruzgan region of Afghanistan has yet to emerge, but it is clear that many people were killed in a US air attack that hit a wedding party. Early confusion may never be entirely resolved, but what is apparent is that the initial statement from the Pentagon gave only a small indication of the full extent of the military operations being undertaken at the time.

At first, it was stated that a coalition reconnaissance aircraft had come under anti-aircraft artillery fire, and that it was a counter-attack by a close air-support aircraft that had resulted in the deaths and injuries. There were, however, subsequent indications that an extensive military operation was under way in the area of the attack, and that this involved US ground troops as well as B-52 and AC-130 aircraft.

Other reports that were published prior to the wedding party attack spoke of a substantial arms find, possibly separate from this operation, involving eight tons of ordnance including missiles. In addition, there was a report some 24 hours earlier that a US location in Afghanistan, probably the base near Kandahar, had been subject to an attack involving rocket-propelled grenades. No casualties were reported.

From the very limited evidence available so far, it seems that a substantial military operation was under way that involved air and ground forces and that it may have met resistance, at least in the form of anti-aircraft fire. Apart from the tragedy for the many people attending the wedding, this does indicate that there is organised resistance to coalition forces, and that this is supported by weapons and munitions still available within Afghanistan.

Once again, the assumption that the war in Afghanistan is over is clearly misplaced, but this has, in any case, been more of a political and media construct. The US military has tended to describe the operations in Afghanistan as 'mopping up', pending the establishment of an effective national Afghan army. However, this is proving more difficult than had been expected. Moreover, there have been firm, if generally unreported, statements that the US armed forces would remain in Afghanistan for at least a year.

Prisoners and war crimes

Beyond the problems in Afghanistan, the wider implications of US security policy post-9/11 are now beginning to emerge, although they will not be made clear until the publication of the National Security Strategy, expected in the early autumn. There have been two early indications of the rigorous commitment to an independent security policy: the controversy over the UN International Criminal Court, which came into being in The Hague this week; and the issue of the treatment of the prisoners held at Guantanamo in Cuba and elsewhere.

In the case of the prisoners, the US Justice Department has argued that a prisoner who is declared an enemy combatant does not have the right to a lawyer, and that it is not appropriate for US lawyers to argue with the classification of such prisoners by the military. The authority to hold such prisoners in US security interests comes from the President, and there appears to be no right of appeal and no limit on the time for which such prisoners can be held in custody.

Justification for this goes back, in part, to the Second World War and such incidents as the internment of thousands of Japanese Americans. It appears to have been extended to include the three US citizens currently being held. It is an argument that has aroused considerable controversy among legal academics, many of whom are concerned with an apparent infringement of liberties that is being extended to US citizens. It is notable, though, that there is a wide variation of opinion, with other legal specialists supporting the Justice Department as part of the necessary war on terror.

The issue of the International Criminal Court is, in one sense, relatively minor, but has considerable implications. The US administration has been consistently antagonistic to the court, an opposition that was strong in Republican circles prior to the 2000 election. The objections are therefore not new, but its current concern is with the possibility of peacekeeping forces being subject to indictment for political motives.

This attitude is substantially different from that of European states, but it is worth remembering that the kind of immunity sought by the US is in line with long-standing assurances given to US forces stationed overseas. One example is the Visiting Forces legislation that has applied to US forces in the UK since the Cold War era.

At the heart of this attitude is a belief that the US systematically acts in a civilised manner that is consonant with western security interests and that it is categorically wrong for its forces to be faced with mischievous actions by those working to other agendas. In its own way, it is as much a reflection of current security thinking as the decision to move more broadly to a posture that embraces pre-emption in the face of new threats.

The pre-history of pre-emptive military action

The changes in the National Security Strategy revolve around the perceived need to act first when the United States is considered to be under threat. It is argued that the Cold War posture was essentially one of 'containing' the Soviet Union by constraining its expansionist policies, and 'deterring' any major offensive action by means of conventional and nuclear forces. This was considered to be appropriate in the context of an organised opposing state operating in a global context and subject to deterrence by virtue of its own vulnerabilities. In other words, the Soviet Union was susceptible to deterrence. Critics of this view would argue that deterrence based on weapons of mass destruction was inherently unwise. They point to what is now known about the Cuban Missile Crisis, the 1983 Able Archer incident and other examples as proof that the Cold War was not at all stable and that we were lucky to get out of it without a catastrophe.

This, though, is only relevant to today's environment in the sense that it shows the lengths to which military strategy is liable to go, and the risks that are taken, to ensure security.

The posture now being developed is based on the belief that 'rogue' states and sub-state paramilitary groups will simply not be deterred in the manner of the Cold War era, and that they must therefore be handled in a much more robust manner, including striking first, even if there is no conclusive evidence of intent to strike the United States or its interests.

Furthermore, such a policy may well extend to pre-empting the use of biological and chemical weapons, even if this involves the use of specialised nuclear weapons such as earth-penetrating warheads.

Is this overall approach new?

It is certainly true that relations with the Soviet Union were, to a large extent, based on mutual deterrence, however risky, but this has not precluded numerous instances of military intervention, some of them involving pre-emption. Panama and Grenada in the 1980s are examples of the latter, and there has been direct or indirect intervention in numerous other countries in Latin America, as well as examples across the Middle East and Asia, not least in Vietnam.

The US change of gear: four sources

Even so, the evolving military posture does represent a much more upfront approach and is being supported by a wide range of military developments across the US armed forces. It also comes at a time when the Bush administration is far less concerned with multilateral agreements, whether these relate to missile defence, nuclear testing, climate change, the weaponisation of space or, indeed, the International Criminal Court.

There have been four substantive elements driving this change, and when they are put together we can get some idea of the sheer momentum of what is happening.

One core element was the development, among the Republican security community in the late 1990s, of a belief that the United States was losing out in its natural post-Cold War world role. Having defeated the Soviet Union, it was now facing myriad lesser threats to its political and economic interests, and it was necessary to be far more forceful in controlling these threats. If the twenty-first century was truly to be the American Century, then this could only come with vigorous political and economic leadership.

A flagship group, the Project for the New American Century, was supported by a galaxy of Republican talent, including Dick Cheney and Donald Rumsfeld. The election of George W. Bush provided the second element – the opportunity to put these ideas into practice.

The third element was the likelihood that such a leadership, with its tough security requirements, would provide a substantial new impetus for the military-industrial complex. While we would not revisit the sudden and massive 'rearming of America' of the early Reagan years, the cutbacks of the 1990s certainly looked to be at an end and prospects for many new projects looked brighter than for a decade.

The final element was, of course, the attacks of 11 September, but what has to be remembered is that these attacks came in the context of a new security agenda that was already being developed. It is for this reason that the response to 9/11 has been particularly tough and wide-ranging.

Furthermore, there remains a clear lack of understanding in Europe and most of the world about the fundamental effects of the attacks. It was not just the human cost of the attacks that was so traumatic, although that was catastrophic for a country that had experienced so little domestic vulnerability. It was that the Twin Towers were remarkable symbols of US international economic influence and their loss went to the heart of the Republican foreign policy agenda.

The United States was shown to be intensely vulnerable just at a time when the prevailing security paradigm was that it was entering a phase of truly global power with no rivals in sight. The response has, therefore, had to be one of an utterly determined policy of regaining and then maintaining control of a deeply volatile international system.

It is this combination of circumstances that is at the heart of the American drive for security, and it is a drive that is likely to result in yet more tension with Europe. It will not go away in the short term and may well survive the 2004 elections, even if they result in a Democrat administration.

The US in the Middle East: playing into the enemy's hands?
17 July 2002

The past fortnight has seen an impressive range of leaks from different parts of the Bush administration, all focusing on a potential war with Iraq. The most dominant of these was the detailed coverage in the *New York Times* (5 July 2002) describing plans for a full-scale invasion intended to destroy the Saddam Hussein regime. There have been other indications, however, that such an option is decidedly unpopular in the State Department and is even viewed with concern in some sectors of the armed forces.

Part of the concern within the military comes from a private acknowledgement that a full-scale war with Iraq could go disastrously wrong, especially if the regime escalates to the use of chemical and biological weapons as it faces destruction.

In the State Department there is a wider concern with the effects of a war on the region. In part, this relates to the fear of a wave of anti-American action, but there is also a concern that a post-Saddam Iraq would fragment into an unstable state. According to this view, Kurdish elements in the north would coalesce with their neighbours in Turkey, causing major problems for the Turkish government, and the Shi'ite communities of southern Iraq would look to Iran, increasing that country's influence in a key part of the Middle East.

A further complication is that some of the various leaks about war with Iraq may have more to do with easing the pressure on President Bush as he faces further probes into the business activities of himself and Vice-President Cheney. Cynics would say that this is the core reason for the leaks and, if they are right, we might well expect a 'mini-crisis' with Iraq in the next few weeks, involving a period of sustained air strikes in response to perceived or actual Iraqi provocation.

The more general questions raised by the leaks relate to how the prospective war with Iraq would link to the conflict with al-Qaida, and its further connection with the continuing Israeli suppression of the Palestinians in the occupied territories. The relevance of broader US attitudes towards the Middle East is also starting to emerge as a key issue.

Forging peace in Afghanistan?

In Afghanistan itself, the formation and training of a national Afghan army is proceeding at a very slow pace, with the important Pashtun ethnic group constituting a very small proportion of the recruits. The drop-out rate of new recruits has been alarmingly high and it is clear that regional warlords retain enormous power and influence.

The President, Hamid Karzai, is evidently working hard to hold the government together, but he is doing it without centralised security forces and has already had to cope with the assassination of a cabinet minister and a Vice-President. He also faces the extraordinary situation where his Defence Minister retains a private army with several hundred armoured vehicles, in the vicinity of Kabul.

The International Security Assistance Force (ISAF) is now led by the Turks but remains a small and lightly armed force of under 5,000, providing little more than a policing presence in and around Kabul. While this has served a valuable purpose, repeated requests to see it increased to around 30,000 and deployed throughout Afghanistan have been blocked by Washington, intent as it is on having free rein for counter-guerrilla operations away from Kabul.

Most such operations are listed as anti-al-Qaida actions, but there is little evidence of al-Qaida activity as the organisation studiously avoids direct contact with foreign Special Forces. Most of the actions are against Taliban groups and associated foreign fighters, with al-Qaida fighters widely dispersed across South-west Asia, and the organisation itself operating in numerous countries. It is noticeable that there have been hardly any arrests of senior al-Qaida members for the best part of four months, in spite of a ready acknowledgement that the organisation remains active.

While there has been some real progress in state-building in a few parts of Afghanistan, including the return of many refugees, the reality is that the international aid programme has been far too small. Efforts to ensure national stability and security have been limited in the extreme compared with what is required. With Washington concentrating excessively on military actions, the much more important task of aiding a return to some form of normality is being missed.

There is a growing feeling among Pashtuns that Hamid Karzai will find it very difficult to deliver any kind of representative administration. This has been heightened by a sense that power resides with ethnic Tajiks and with warlords, together with a bitterness over the US raid on 1 July that killed 48 civilians at a wedding party and injured over 120.

This appears to have had little effect on Washington, not least because US troops in Afghanistan are experiencing problems that are not widely reported outside the country. Since the 1 July incident, there have been three reported attacks on US units. Two were near Kandahar, with each injuring a US soldier. More recently a US

Special Forces base came under fire from small arms and rocket-propelled grenades, but there were no casualties.

These incidents reinforce the view in Washington that continued Special Forces operations, backed by air power, are essential. They take precedence over state-building and may involve long-term military commitments.

Bush's free hand for Israel

Some weeks after President Bush's speech on Israel and the Palestinians, it is evident that the Sharon government has seen it as an opportunity to use a free hand in the West Bank and Gaza. This has involved the further development of what amounts to an open prison of 1 million people in Gaza, with an increasing number of them impoverished and supported by UNRWA (United Nations Relief and Works Agency) and other agencies.

It has also resulted in the control of most of the key towns and cities of the West Bank by the Israeli army. It has caused renewed hardship right across the territories, leading to concern within governments across Europe but little or no criticism from Washington.

An indication of Sharon's determination to enforce control of the occupied territories is the appointment of General Moshe Ya'alon as the new Chief of General Staff. Ya'alon, a former paratrooper, previously served as head of military intelligence and of Israel's Central Command which controls the West Bank. His predecessor, General Shaul Mofaz, is a noted hawk who believes that Palestinian paramilitaries must be controlled by military force. Mofaz could well be a future Defence Minister and Ya'alon is expected to follow his policy of rigorous military control.

In the wider region, while Israeli policy has further incensed opinion across most of the Middle East, some of the key governments have been notably silent on the issue. The underlying reason for this may have a significance that transcends the immediate confrontation between the Israelis and Palestinians, although current Israeli actions are virtually certain to result in a further violent response against their own people.

US security policy in the region

The more we look at President Bush's speech, the more we see an attitude taking root that indicates the overall approach of the administration to the region. What it appears to be about is a belief that the problems of the region can be controlled by means of three approaches – working with the elites of selected states, rigorous support for Israel and its hard-line treatment of the Palestinians, and the use of US military force when required.

The major such requirement is the termination of the Saddam Hussein regime. This is seen as a fundamental necessity. It is not so much that such a 'rogue state' cannot be allowed to exist in such a geopolitically important region; it is, rather, that states considered to be enemies of the United States simply cannot be allowed to develop their own weapons of mass destruction.

This strategy actually has a further element in that if the Saddam Hussein regime is ended, it will demonstrate unequivocally that the US and its allies are in control, discouraging other regimes from following a similar path. In every sense, then, the Iraqi regime has to go. It may take time, and there may be a dispute over how to do it, but it is necessary that it be done.

Apart from support for Israel, the other element in the US strategy appears to be a ready willingness to work with the elites of a number of states in the region, most notably Kuwait, Saudi Arabia and Jordan. While the Saudi leadership is very cautious in its dealings with Washington, it is also acutely conscious of the opposition within its own population, and would prefer, on balance, to see the Iraqi regime fall.

Washington's support for certain regimes needs to be seen in the context of the political illegitimacy of most of the regimes in the region. If one element of dissent in the region is the continuing action of the Israeli government, the other is far less clear-cut but nevertheless endemic. This is the deep division between ruling elites and their associates on the one hand, and large sectors of their populations, including huge numbers of educated but disengaged and frustrated young people, on the other.

The elites are generally aware of this, but largely fail to address it, and it is for this reason that they are prepared to accept US influence and support, not least in the interests of their own security. Washington, meanwhile, sees a potential axis of support involving the apparently disparate elements of a hard-line Israeli government and some key elites in the Gulf states.

On such a basis, it believes that its own massive military power can be used effectively to deal with Iraq, and that subsequent actions can ensure a stable region. Control, in short, can be maintained, Israel can be secure, the immense oil reserves of the region remain available and the activities of the terrorist networks can be limited.

Can it work? The short answer, given US military strength and political determination coupled with the concerns of regional ruling elites, is that it may appear to – at least for the time being. Thus the Israelis will control Palestinian militants by force, military action will be taken against Iraq and stability will be ensured. It takes little account of the risk of an escalating war involving weapons of mass destruction, for that is seen as a necessary risk in the circumstances.

There is, though, another and much greater problem that does not seem to enter the minds of the key strategists in the Bush administration, at least outside of some of the thoughtful people in the State Department. This is that such a policy is precisely what paramilitary groups such as al-Qaida actually want.

Over the next few months we can see the prospect of firm control of the Palestinians by an Israeli government very close to Washington. This will be coupled with the careful nurturing of connections with selected ruling elites, especially in the western Gulf states, and the build-up of substantial military forces in the region.

From the point of view of al-Qaida, it is a near-perfect scenario, calculated impressively to give it far greater financial and personal support across much of the region. Anti-American and anti-elite sentiments will grow, leading to the strengthening of al-Qaida and the development of similar groups.

In the short term, Washington may believe that the US can maintain control and deal with Iraq. In the long term it is setting up precisely those forces that will lead to formidable problems that will actually increase its own insecurity.

What appears to be a potentially successful strategy for maintaining control of a strategically crucial part of the world is actually a strategy more likely to end in a loss of control and greater risks to US interests, both abroad and at home.

Israel, the US and the world: a conflict of perceptions
24 July 2002

Since the start of the latest Palestinian Intifada nearly two years ago, Israel's armed forces have been heavily committed to actions in towns and cities of the West Bank, while maintaining control of Gaza and taking a range of military actions in southern Lebanon. Reservists have had to be called up several times and the current deployments involve the virtual reoccupation of the West Bank.

Until last week, the garrisoning of these urban areas was expected to be short-lived, but the recent suicide bombings and shootings have strengthened the determination of the Sharon government to continue with its hard-line security measures. There is, as yet, no evidence of any recognition that these measures are actually adding to Israel's insecurity, and the appointment of General Ya'alon as the new Chief of General Staff confirms the current hard-line stance.

Although almost all the emphasis is on military operations in the territories directly controlled by Israel, the Israeli Defence Forces (IDF) have a much wider concern, much of it relating to regional antagonists such as Syria, Iraq and Iran. As such, the IDF are constantly seeking new and upgraded equipment to meet new perceived threats. Instead, it is found that an increasing part of the defence budget is going on operational costs at the expense of research, development and the production of new weapons.

Even so, Israel is maintaining a very high defence budget, is receiving substantial aid from the United States, and is involved in a range of new military developments. An examination of these gives us some idea of the Israeli military view of the Middle East, and of the manner in which the IDF and Israeli defence industries are so intertwined with their US counterparts.

The logic of proliferation

Israeli military thinking commonly envisages Israel as being surrounded by three 'rings' of potentially or actually hostile countries. The first ring includes Syria, Egypt and Jordan. Although the latter two are not currently considered hostile, Israel has been at war with them in the past and the military still treat them with some circumspection. Beyond them lies the second ring, including Iraq and Libya, with the third ring currently involving Iran.

From the Israeli point of view, there is little substantial threat from conventional armed forces, either crossing borders or staging air attacks, as Israel believes it can cope with these. What is of much greater concern is the proliferation of missiles and the fear that they might be equipped with chemical, biological or even nuclear weapons.

Israel itself has by far the strongest such forces in the region, including well over 100 nuclear weapons that can either be dropped as free-fall bombs by strike aircraft or can be carried as warheads on the Jericho II ballistic missile. Israel may well also have chemical and biological weapons.

Even so, it does not see these as representing a threat to other states in the region, and does not accept in any way that its possession of such weapons is a stimulus to other states to develop their own weapons of mass destruction. These are not seen as deterrents, whereas Israel considers that its own forces are just that.

In a sense, this is a part of a common problem of 'mirror-imaging', what international security analysts term the security dilemma – make yourself strong and your opponent does the same, so you make yourself stronger.

In Israel's case there is a further reason, in that the trauma of Iraq's Scud missile attacks on Israel during the 1991 Gulf War have had an enduring impact. That the major population centres of Israel could be attacked, albeit by crude Scud missiles, had a lasting effect on Israeli military thinking. It has led to repeated examples of worst-case scenarios in their forward planning.

Even so, here again, the issue is seen solely from an Israeli perspective. There is no recognition that other states see Israel as aggressive, with its repeated actions in Lebanon, past attacks against targets as far away as Tunisia and Iraq, and assassinations and other actions across the world.

The US commonly exaggerates its predictions on issues such as missile proliferation, just as it tended to overplay the strength of the Soviet military during the Cold War. Currently, Israel takes this much further even than the US. It contends, for example, that Iran's new Shahab II missile, with a range of 1,300 kilometres, has completed its early tests, that up to two dozen have already been deployed and that it will go into a production run of up to 150 missiles. Furthermore, it believes Iran will have its first nuclear weapon within three years, whereas the US view is more like five years.

The Israeli view is that Syria is upgrading its Scud missiles with a new version that can reach the whole of Israel from launchers in remote parts of north-east Syria that are difficult to attack. There is even a view that Libya is developing a missile that may be a version of the North Korean No Dong missile, and may have up to 100 of these within eight years.

Israel feels insecure

This security mentality is rarely recognised outside Israel, except in Washington, and the prevailing view is of an Israel that is concerned only with its problems in the territories it directly controls. The latter may dominate the public mood in Israel, and is largely why Sharon maintains support for remarkably hard-line policies that most analysts outside Israel see as self-defeating – 'watering the seeds of terror' as it has been called.

But it has to be remembered that while outside perceptions may see a remarkably strong Israel rigorously controlling the Palestinians, the Israeli military see themselves surrounded by opposing states. These, however weak, are seen to be developing weapons that can reach Israel, and they therefore require military responses that may well involve pre-emption.

In part, these responses involve a range of new ground-based early-warning radar systems, airborne early warning AWACS planes, and anti-ballistic missiles. The US is intimately involved in most of these programmes; Israel currently fields improved US Patriot missile batteries and has developed its own Arrow ballistic missile defence system with close US industrial involvement. Israel's new AWACS plane is the US General Dynamics Gulfstream V, with six on order, as well as three more to be modified as intelligence gathering and targeting aircraft.

Israel is also determined to have the means to attack states that may be able to deploy missiles carrying weapons of mass destruction, and also to pre-empt such developments by attacking production facilities, much as it did in 1981 when it bombed Iraq's Osiraq nuclear reactor.

One recent decision that relates to this was the order for 100 new F-16I aircraft. These are developed and built in the US specifically to meet Israeli air force requirements for long-range strike aircraft that can accompany the larger F-15I planes that are already deployed.

The US and Israel: a lengthy intimacy

An indication of the close connections with the US has been shown by the co-operation involved in the interception of the *Karine A* earlier this year. This was the merchant ship that was boarded by Israeli forces en route from Iran, with a cargo that included 50 tons of arms that Israel believed were destined for Palestinian forces.

The *Karine A* was originally tracked from the Persian Gulf across the North Arabian Sea by US Navy P-3 maritime reconnaissance aircraft. Although the Israelis initially lost contact with the ship when it called into the Yemeni port of Hudaydah, they reacquired it as it entered the Red Sea, using an experimental spy plane based on a Boeing 737 airframe. This uses equipment that will be mounted in the Gulfstream V aircraft mentioned above.

Thus, in the *Karine A* case, US-acquired equipment and close US military co-operation was directly involved in the whole process, an aspect of the relationship that extends across many areas of military activity.

This co-operation with Israel stretches back to the 1950s. After its establishment in 1948, Israel was not initially allied to the US in any substantial way, at least not at the level of governmental aid. With the rise of Arab nationalism in the 1950s, and the intrusion of the Cold War into the region, this was to change. While links with France and other countries were maintained, it was the US that increasingly saw Israel as the bulwark of its security posture in the region.

This situation was to last throughout the rest of the Cold War, and there was concern that the end of the Soviet threat would lead to Israel's importance to Washington being downgraded. To an extent this happened during the 1990s, but the attacks of 11 September and the subsequent war on terror have resulted in a return to the close relationship of previous years.

Perhaps the clearest example of the closeness of this relationship is the recent Israeli request for more than 2,000 anti-armour missiles worth $80 million. Sale of these Raytheon TOW 2A anti-armour missiles was approved by the Bush administration in late June, following an Israeli request for urgent action.

According to the IDF, the missiles are for use 'against armour, combat vehicles and other manoeuvrable elements', but, as *Jane's Defence Weekly* reported last week, the IDF has actually been using the missiles repeatedly in air and ground attacks against Palestinian targets, such as buildings.

Some indication of the intensity of recent IDF operations in the West Bank is given by an IDF statement that more weapons and munitions have been used in the past three months than in the last decade in all its operations, including those in Lebanon.

Same reality, different outlooks

The US once again sees Israel as its crucial ally in the region – no longer (as during the Cold War) an assistant in the war on communism, but rather a key part of the war on terror, with Palestinian militants seen as one part of the wider threat.

In the region as a whole, Israel is now viewed as a small but extraordinarily strong country determined to use any means to maintain its security, including wholesale repression of the Palestinians in the occupied territories. Furthermore, it is seen as locked into US policies, equipped by US arms companies and working closely with the US military.

Israel, on the other hand, sees itself as a country threatened by terror groups bent on its destruction. This view is shared to a very large extent in Washington. Furthermore, Israel's sense of encirclement by rogue states and hostile groups fuels its perceived requirement for highly potent offensive forces. These perceptions, of threat and of the necessary capacities needed to handle it, feed readily into the more radical paramilitary organisations in the region, especially al-Qaida.

What is important to appreciate is that Israel's treatment of the Palestinians may be deeply counterproductive and ultimately disastrous for its own security, but it is part of an absolute determination to maintain control. Moreover, and this is what outside analysts tend to forget, it is part of a wider outlook that regards this remarkably powerful yet small country as isolated and at risk.

Outside Israel, the country may be seen as aggressive, militarily superior, and with the world's sole superpower behind it. In Israel itself, in contrast, the 'David versus Goliath' image persists. This conflict of perceptions, in which the country's close relationship with the United States plays a key role, is one of the core reasons why Israelis find it so difficult to achieve a more realistic view of their country's situation.

Meanwhile in Afghanistan ...
4 September 2002

Last week, a draft United Nations report confirmed what had been suspected by a number of analysts, that it was proving very difficult to control the al-Qaida network's movement of funds and that it was successfully gaining access to substantial additional funds, sufficient to finance further attacks. In the months immediately following 11 September, $112 million was blocked. But barely $10 million more has been intercepted over the past eight months.

Al-Qaida and its associated groups have been able to use a wide range of banking systems, increasingly augmented by the use of the *halawa* informal money-lending networks. They have also made extensive use of gold and gems as means of transferring resources between countries.

As the first anniversary of the attacks approaches, there has been a predictably strong reaction from the Bush administration. According to officials, the war on terror is going well: al-Qaida is crippled and operations in Afghanistan amount to little more than a process of 'mopping up'.

Hotfoot on this announcement, however, came an attempted hijacking of a Ryanair jet in Stockholm. The details remain unclear, especially as to whether the putative hijacker was acting alone or was part of a larger group. At the very least there appears to have been an informal connection with other incidents. In any case, if there was no direct connection with al-Qaida, it may well illustrate one problem that is facing the United States and its associates – that there is a more general capacity for anti-US groups and individuals to engage in attacks.

The early focus on Osama bin Laden as the central figure of power, and the view of al-Qaida as a rigorously organised hierarchical group, was always a dangerous simplification, dangerous because it under-

estimated the particular nature of the problem. A single rigid organisation, even one operating in a number of countries, is relatively
vulnerable to counteraction. A much more loose network of groups
and even individuals, sharing a common purpose directed against the
United States, is a much more difficult phenomenon to counter.

The al-Qaida group and its Taliban associates nevertheless remain
the most significant part of this orientation. Amid the conflicting
reports on its current status, is it possible to get a reasonably accurate
idea of the position of the organisation and of the security position
in Afghanistan?

Insecurity in Afghanistan

In the past three weeks, a certain amount of information has entered
the public domain that helps us to do this, much of it building on trends
that have become apparent over the past three months. Taken together,
they support the view that Afghanistan is deeply unstable and that
there is a considerable risk that it will slip back into civil war and
wholesale disorder.

This is at a time when more than a million refugees have returned
home, and some semblance of civil society is developing, especially
in Kabul. It would be tragic if, primarily because of a fundamental
lack of international commitment to support for post-conflict peace-
building, this progress were lost.

The evidence for developing problems comes from many sources
and covers a range of factors. As previously discussed, it is proving
very difficult to create an effective Afghan national army. There are
wide-ranging problems of warlordism, and opium production has
increased.

There have been a number of incidents of bombings and attempted
bombings in Kabul, including a massive car bomb that was intercepted by accident after a minor traffic incident. In recent weeks there
have been further bomb attacks, one of them injuring a British soldier
serving with the International Security Assistance Force (ISAF) in
Kabul at the weekend.

This week alone, a bomb exploded outside the old Soviet embassy,
killing one person and injuring three, and two land mines exploded
near the Bagram base, killing four and injuring 18.

There remains an enduring power struggle between the President, Hamid Karzai, and the ambitious Defence Minister, Mohammed Fahim, who maintains what is effectively a private army of several thousand Tajik militia fighters drawn mainly from the Panjshir Valley in north-eastern Afghanistan. This struggle persists, following the assassination of a cabinet minister and of Vice-President Abdul Kazir earlier in the year.

The US military presence

If these factors illustrate the instability at the heart of Afghan politics, what is more worrying for the United States is the increase in tensions involving its own troops in the country, now numbering some 10,000. There is, furthermore, a suspicion that only a small proportion of attacks on US forces are being reported.

Here and there, some information seeps out. Two weeks ago, some 2,000 US and coalition troops conducted one of the largest search operations of the war in south-eastern Afghanistan. Operation Mountain Sweep was intended to kill or capture numerous Taliban and al-Qaida guerrilla units operating in a range of villages and towns.

The eight-day operation was a failure. The entire process yielded a vanload of weapons, two caches of documents and ten prisoners, with every indication that the entire operation had been thoroughly compromised. There is a suspicion that guerrilla forces had indeed been present in the area, but had had ample warning of the operation and had moved on to other locations.

Al-Qaida claims that it has penetrated the major coalition operating bases such as Bagram Air Base north of Kabul, and that it has support in much of the country, but especially in the Pashtun areas. These claims are quietly accepted by senior US military in the country, as is the fact that guerrilla units have active supply lines and ample logistical support, both made easier through operating in parts of Afghanistan where there is deep-seated antagonism to US forces.

One of the major independent strategic analysis groups in the US is the Houston-based Stratfor, which works for a range of business clients and has a reasonable reputation for its analytical independence. In a recent and very sobering assessment of the situation in Afghanistan, it claimed that US forces on the ground are experiencing far greater security problems than is publicly acknowledged.

Sources say that there are nightly attacks on U.S. troops, which is confirmed by non-governmental organizations in the country, who add that increased restrictions have been placed on the movements of off-duty U.S. forces. U.S. troops reportedly control only the towns where they have bases, and then only in daylight, while the Karzai government reportedly controls only parts of Kabul. (Stratfor, 28 August 2002)

Stratfor's assessment does fit in with other indications. Even the mainstream international press reported at least five significant attacks on US units during July. There have been a number of more recent bombing incidents before this week's incidents, including one at the Communications Ministry in Kabul on 15 August and another intercepted 500 metres from the US embassy on 20 August.

One of the US Special Forces soldiers injured in an earlier attack has since died and there are reports from a number of sources that suggest that the US forces have suffered a significant number of casualties, including many soldiers killed. These reports persist but are denied by the Pentagon.

What is more widely recognised is that there has been an upsurge in popular opposition to the US military presence, exacerbated by the deaths of civilians in air strikes, with this spreading across most of the Pashtun provinces.

All of these aspects do not add up to the resurgence of major guerrilla warfare, at least not yet, but there are indications that the al-Qaida organisation now sees an opportunity to operate once more in Afghanistan, especially in those areas close to the Pakistan border.

A role for Britain? Three options: not two

There have been repeated calls from the UN and from Mr Karzai himself for a substantial increase in support, not least with the aim of extending ISAF to a strength of 30,000, enabling it to operate in many more cities and towns and to aid transport and communications. While the Bush administration has been strongly opposed to this until recently, there is some recognition even in Washington that the situation is deteriorating.

British Special Forces and Commandos were involved fairly substantially in Afghanistan, although the Marine Commando deployment in the spring resulted in few interceptions in spite of intensive operations. Where Britain has played a genuinely more constructive role has been in its support for ISAF and also in a range of civil assistance programmes.

One option for Britain would be to substantially increase its commitment to post-conflict security and reconstruction, building on some reasonable efforts already underway. This might include a willingness to contribute up to two-thirds of the 30,000 troops that ISAF really needs, coupled with a substantial increase in aid for health, education, transport and other projects.

A major and sustained commitment to ISAF, it could be argued, would be a far more valuable role for Britain to play than to get involved in the US war against Iraq. Indeed, a large-scale commitment to Afghanistan would mean that the UK would not have the capacity to operate in Iraq as well, as that would overstretch the limited forces Britain has available.

In facing up to the dilemma over the Bush plan for war against Iraq, the UK actually has three options, not two. The obvious ones are that it could back Washington to the hilt, with all the dangers that this involves, or it could oppose the war forcefully. The latter looks frankly unlikely, however widely that might be supported domestically.

The third approach, the 'Afghanistan Option', is to stay out of the war with Iraq but develop a greatly increased commitment to supporting a peaceful transition for Afghanistan. It is an approach that Washington refuses to take up, but there is no reason why that has to apply to the UK, especially if it works in coalition with European and regional associates.

Such an approach has two advantages. One is that it could be genuinely valuable in facilitating a transition to a much more peaceful and stable Afghanistan. The other is that it could mean that the UK can still have some influence with Washington without getting involved in a highly dangerous war in the Middle East. Given the hard-line nature of the Bush security advisers on this issue, a moderating influence in Washington might not go amiss in the coming months.

After Bali, the need to understand
16 October 2002

Although the major focus of security analysts in recent months has been on the US policy towards Iraq and the probability of war within three to four months, some observers have also been concentrating their concern on developments in Afghanistan and the evolution of al-Qaida and its associates.

Indeed, within UK intelligence circles there is said to be a common view that the US determination to terminate the Saddam Hussein regime has become so central that other developments are being missed.

Since the massacre in Bali four days ago, this view has become more widespread. But if we are to get a deeper idea of what is really happening, we need to look at a number of events and developments of the past two weeks, perhaps best placed in the context of earlier analyses concerning Afghanistan and al-Qaida.

Yemen, Kuwait, Pakistan ... and US plans for Iraq

There are four incidents, in addition to the bombings in Bali, which are particularly relevant. The first is the attempt to destroy the French supertanker *Limburg* off the coast of Yemen. The method of this attack was very similar to that employed in the assault on the USS *Cole* missile destroyer in Aden harbour, South Yemen, almost exactly two years ago, which killed 17 US sailors and caused $350 million of damage.

Initially the Yemeni authorities denied that the *Limburg* had been attacked, stating that there had been an on-board explosion, but this is now discounted. What is perhaps more significant is that the tanker survived the attack primarily because it was of recent construction involving the 'double hull' design. This gives a tanker much greater resilience, whereas an older tanker could well have been destroyed in the attack.

The second incident occurred two days after the *Limburg* incident, when a pair of gunmen fired on two groups of US Marines training on Failaka Island off the Kuwaiti coast. One Marine was shot dead and another injured before the attackers were killed. The incident has caused dismay among US officials in the region, not least as it now appears that the assailants had direct links with al-Qaida and had trained in Afghanistan.

The latter remains to be seen, but what is really remarkable is that the attackers were able to get firearms on to the tightly controlled island, acquire a pickup truck and then breach a secure training area. Such an attack is simply not meant to happen, and indicates that US troops in Kuwait, ostensibly a supportive state, are actually at risk long before a war with Iraq starts.

The third incident is the recent success of the United Action Forum in elections in Pakistan, especially in western provinces, not least in the North-West Frontier Province where it gained a majority of seats in the legislative assembly. Although the Forum denies links with al-Qaida, it has campaigned vigorously on the basis of opposition to US involvement in the region. Its success does not present a substantial threat to President Musharraf's firm control of Pakistan but it does demonstrate the extent of popular antagonism to US policies.

The fourth incident takes us away from al-Qaida and back to Iraq. It relates to reliable reports (for example in the *International Herald Tribune*) that US action subsequent to the intended destruction of the Saddam Hussein regime now leans towards the military occupation of Iraq, pending the eventual establishment of some kind of client regime.

Such an occupying force would clearly include substantial numbers of US troops, entail a protracted search for any weapons systems that had been hidden by the current regime, and also involve the renovation of the Iraqi oil production facilities. This, in turn, would ensure that US enterprises have a dominant role in the development of Iraq's oil reserves – the largest in the world after Saudi Arabia.

Al-Qaida spider, American fly?

If we now put these four incidents into the wider context of the activities of al-Qaida over the past year, we can get a sharper awareness of what is happening world-wide.

It remains the case that few members of the al-Qaida leadership have been killed or captured, and that its dispersal from Afghanistan was a setback but was by no means unexpected.

Moreover, al-Qaida is best seen as part of a much wider and quite loose alliance of radical movements, although it has a central role for many other groups, not least in terms of training and finance. Al-Qaida, and its associates, have been remarkably active, even before the recent attacks. These have included attempts against US embassies in Paris and Rome, at least one attempt to destroy a passenger jet, an attack on the US Consulate in Karachi, the killing of French naval technicians in the same city, attacks in Islamabad, the attempt to shoot down a USAF plane in Saudi Arabia, the bombing of the Tunisian synagogue and many more.

Perhaps most significant was the interception by the Singapore security forces of a plan to use several powerful truck bombs against the financial district of that city. This may have been planned in parallel with an attack on the airport at Changi, a key hub for South-east Asia.

What this all means is that the assumption that destroying the Taliban regime and disrupting al-Qaida in Afghanistan would greatly limit its capabilities was plainly wrong. If anything, the 'war on terror' of the past year may even have strengthened support for the organisation and its associates, support which is further boosted by continuing Israeli actions on the West Bank and in Gaza. While these have slipped away from the headlines in the western press, they are reported in detail in the Middle East and Asia.

Indeed, one small item of news, so far missed in the western press, is that the United States has offered the Israeli government 24 hours' notice of an attack on Iraq (*Defense News*, 14 October 2002). From an American point of view this makes good sense, not least as a tactic for helping to keep Israel out of the war, but throughout the Middle East it will be seen as further proof, if any were needed, of the intricate links between the US and Israel.

It is in this context that the US plan to occupy Iraq should be seen. Again, from Washington's perspective this makes sense – there is no point in destroying the regime only to see Iraq come apart in chaos. But from the perspective of al-Qaida, it merely proves their point; Iraq may be a secular regime but it is still primarily an Arab state and US occupation would be proof of one of al-Qaida's long-term arguments – that Washington, along with Israel, seeks control of the region.

Indeed, there is an argument that one of the aims of the 9/11 atrocities was precisely to draw the United States more fully into the region. This has already happened in Afghanistan and in Central Asia – an American occupation of Iraq would, from al-Qaida's perspective, be as close to a dream result as it could wish for.

Don't just condemn, understand

This brings us back to the terrible events in Bali. Exactly who was responsible, and the extent of the connections with al-Qaida, may remain unclear for a long time, but one effect of the atrocity will be to renew a commitment to the war on terror – a war conducted primarily by military means.

This is understandable and should be expected – indeed it may be that one of the purposes of the attack was precisely this result. It is difficult to say this at a time of such suffering and loss of life, but if we respond solely by trying to redouble efforts to destroy al-Qaida and its associates, the effect may be simply to strengthen their support.

What we are still failing to do is to understand the root causes of the support for such movements. To seek to understand is not to condone in any shape or form, but it does raise the possibility of recognising the reasons for their enduring support and, in turn, offering some prospect for undercutting it.

The problem is that this different angle of vision would go right to the heart of policy towards Israel as well as the wider issues of the western control of the Gulf region. The Bush administration is not remotely prepared to entertain such a consideration – it has to come from elsewhere.

Is al-Qaida winning?
7 November 2002

Fourteen months after the attacks on New York and Washington, what is the state of the 'war on terror'? It is particularly appropriate to ask this now, with so much of the attention being focused on Iraq, including the imminent call-up of reserves for the British armed forces.

Any effort to undertake an independent analysis of the progress of this other war comes to some uncomfortable conclusions, so much so that when analysts do so, there is a tendency to shoot the messenger rather than listen to the message.

Afghanistan

Take Afghanistan first. The Taliban regime was dispersed rather than destroyed, with the United States using rearmed Northern Alliance forces as its ground troops, in combination with the extensive use of air power, the latter killing some thousands of Afghan civilians in the process. Many Taliban elements melted away into their own villages and towns in Afghanistan or Pakistan, with their weapons intact. During the war itself, there were few occasions when Taliban militia were engaged in open combat – in most cases they simply retreated.

There were even fewer occasions when al-Qaida militia were engaged in combat, and there remain suspicions that many of them may have even dispersed before 11 September last year. Certainly, whenever al-Qaida training camps were occupied by US or other forces, they were found to be deserted.

Repeated attempts in recent months to target Taliban and other militias have failed, and even large-scale operations such as Clean Sweep, involving about 2,000 US and local troops supported by air power, have failed to capture or kill more than a handful of militia members.

Only a small proportion of the Taliban and al-Qaida leadership have been killed or taken into custody and the great majority of the inmates of Camp X-Ray have turned out to be lower-level operatives, with many now being released.

Within Afghanistan itself, the International Security Assistance Force has brought some stability to Kabul, but in much of the rest of the country, warlordism has returned with a vengeance, often aided by the flood of light arms cascading through the country as a result of the rearming of the Northern Alliance and other groups opposed to the Taliban last year.

Some countries have provided assistance, not least Britain, and India's recent substantial loan offer is welcome, but realistic international aid for state building has been woefully inadequate, putting President Karzai's administration in some difficulty. This is made worse by problems with attempting to create a national Afghan army, and by the presence of private armies controlled by individual ministers, especially the Minister of Defence, General Mohammed Fahim.

In recent months, a cabinet minister and a Vice-President have been assassinated and there have been two assassination attempts against President Karzai, who is now guarded by US Special Forces. This week, President Karzai sacked a number of regional officials, primarily on the grounds of corruption, but he has refrained from taking on the more powerful warlords, many of whom are gaining from revenues accruing from the rapid increase in opium production.

Perhaps most worrying are the indications that Taliban forces are reorganising along the Pakistan border, a process that may have been made easier by the recent successes of Islamic parties in elections in the Pakistani provinces bordering Afghanistan. In one significant development, reported in the *International Herald Tribune* (4 November), Pentagon officials say that while some of the recently uncovered weapons caches were those left behind by retreating Taliban forces, 'some are fresh caches planted by units preparing guerrilla attacks against the government of President Karzai'.

Al-Qaida

If the situation in Afghanistan is problematic, the status of al-Qaida should cause even more concern. This is an organisation that was supposed to have been dispersed and thoroughly disrupted by a combination of the war on Afghanistan, numerous arrests across the world and the extensive co-operation of security and intelligence agencies in numerous countries.

There certainly has been disruption or prevention of some major operations including:

- planned attacks on US embassies in Rome and Paris;
- an attempt to shoot down a US warplane in Saudi Arabia using a portable surface-to-air missile;
- a plan to attack western warships in the Straits of Gibraltar;
- the attempted bombing of a US passenger jet;
- a plan to develop radiological weapons for use in the United States; and
- a major attack in Singapore using multiple powerful truck bombs, possibly aimed at embassies and the financial district.

From what is known of the Singapore operation, it would have been on the scale of the 9/11 attacks, might also have involved an attack on Changi Airport and would have had a profound economic impact as well as a great human cost.

It can certainly be argued that the very fact that these operations were all prevented means that al-Qaida must be in retreat, yet the very fact that they were attempted means that the organisation and its associates have been seeking to maintain a level of activity that is actually higher than the period prior to 9/11.

In any case, what is even more significant is the catalogue of actual attacks:

- a bomb attack on the US consulate in Karachi;
- the shooting of worshippers at the church in the diplomatic compound in Islamabad;
- the killing of French naval technicians in Karachi;
- the killing of Christian aid workers in Pakistan;
- the attack on the synagogue in Tunisia, killing German tourists and local people;
- the killing of a US Special Forces soldier in the Philippines and two major bomb attacks in the same country;
- a bomb attack on a French oil tanker off the Yemeni coast;
- last weekend's attack on a US oil company's helicopter taking off from Sana'a Airport in Yemen;
- the murder of a US diplomat in Amman;
- two attacks on US Marines in a secure training area in Kuwait; and
- the devastating bomb attack on the Sari nightclub in Bali.

It is when these are all put together, as so rarely happens, that one gets some idea of the extent of the activity. By no means all of these are actions directly carried out by the al-Qaida network – a number of them may be down to local groups working in no more than a loose affiliation with al-Qaida. The point is that these attacks are now happening almost weekly, in several different countries, and they collectively suggest that the anti-American and anti-western mood is showing no signs whatsoever of diminishing.

Furthermore, the al-Qaida organisation itself appears to have developed a more dispersed leadership, with as many as six significant people involved. It is maintaining support in many countries and is successfully moving financial and other resources around the world.

Prospects

For western analysts seeking an overview, it is not a promising picture, and there are two factors that may further increase support for al-Qaida and its associates. One is the current political crisis in Israel, notably the withdrawal of the Labour Party from Sharon's coalition. Whatever the outcome of the current upheavals, the most likely result will be the adoption of more hard-line policies towards the Palestinians as Israel moves further to the right.

Although al-Qaida has had little or no involvement with the Palestinian cause, it gains regional support every time that Israel takes military action in the occupied territories. This extends to further opposition to the United States, which is seen as Israel's sponsor and champion in the region.

The other factor, inevitably, is the coming war with Iraq. Here again, al-Qaida and its associates have little or no connection with the secular Iraqi regime, but the movement of substantial US forces into the region, and the impending operation to terminate the Iraqi regime, is seen as a veritable proof of al-Qaida's oft-repeated claim that the United States and its western allies are determined to control the region.

In such circumstances it is hardly surprising that Saudi Arabia is once again dubious about allowing the US armed forces to use its territory for an attack on Iraq. Nor should it be a surprise that the Kuwaiti authorities have just closed down the offices of the independent and very popular Al-Jazeera TV network in Kuwait City. According to the BBC, a senior Kuwaiti government official said the closure was due to a 'lack of professionalism and neutrality when dealing with Kuwait issues'. He denied that it was a matter of censorship – 'I would stress Kuwait's belief in democracy and freedom', he said.

As far as the future of the 'war on terror' is concerned, an overall picture is emerging of a loose alliance of anti-American and anti-

western groups, many of them connected to al-Qaida, but collectively active in a number of countries. The frequency of the attacks
indicates a level of activity that may actually be on the increase, and
it certainly does appear to be the case that support for such groups
is at least as strong as 14 months ago, and very probably stronger.
On that basis, any talk of the 'war on terror' being a success is a very
long way from reality.

Lessons from Mombasa: al-Qaida's long-term strategy
4 December 2002

An earlier analysis of the status of al-Qaida (7 November 2002)
came to the conclusion that the organisation had experienced
disruption in Afghanistan and a number of recent reversals but was,
on balance, more active than 18 months ago. While major attacks in
Paris, Rome, Singapore and elsewhere had been prevented, their
very planning demonstrated the power of the organisation and its
affiliates. Moreover, many other attacks had succeeded in their aims
– not least the Bali bombing, the attack on the Tunisian synagogue,
several bombings in Pakistan and assaults in Yemen.

One overall conclusion that could be drawn from these developments was that al-Qaida was not a monolithic and hierarchical
organisation with one small group of key leaders directing every
operation anywhere in the world. Rather, the al-Qaida phenomenon
is best seen as an association of like-minded groups operating in
many countries with some loose co-ordination, with more centralised
training and financing, and technical expertise, available when
required.

Within this wider organisation, al-Qaida may be the most significant group and it may have a strategic sense of direction that provides
some long-term co-ordination, but the removal of its most senior
leadership would not in any sense bring the numerous paramilitary
actions to an end.

For the US, a harsher climate

If this is a reasonably accurate assessment of the position a month
ago, what is the position in the aftermath of the bombing of the

Israeli-owned Paradise Hotel near Mombasa and the attempt to destroy an Israeli charter airliner taking off from the nearby airport?

The first point to make is that this was actually one of a series of recent developments. In Pakistan, following the provincial elections, a radical Islamic leader, Akram Khan Durrani, was last week elected chief minister of the North-West Frontier Province. This followed the success of his United Action Forum religious coalition in elections held on 10 October. The coalition has a 32-seat majority over all other parties in the 124-seat assembly and Durrani has come to power with policies that include the strengthening of Islamic law and also the exclusion of US troops from the province.

In another development, the trial began this week in Rotterdam of four men accused of planning attacks on the US embassy in Paris and on the Kleine-Brogel Air Force Base in Belgium, which includes a US munitions store. The trial relates to activities being planned before 11 September 2001, indicating the extent of other operations that were already under development.

Elsewhere, there was a further shooting incident directed against US soldiers in Kuwait when two soldiers were wounded by a junior Kuwaiti police officer. This was the latest in a string of incidents in Kuwait, including the killing of a US Marine last month, and one result has been the sacking of the head of security in Kuwait. In Lebanon, a young American evangelist, Bonnie Witherall, was killed at the clinic in Sidon where she worked as a nurse. Lebanese security officials were reported as saying that they thought the murder was linked to the anti-American mood that is prevalent across so much of the Middle East.

In their different ways, these four examples serve as a reminder of two aspects of the 'war on terror'. First, there is the extent of the anti-American mood that is rampant throughout the Middle East and South-west Asia, a mood which is much harsher than before the attacks on New York and Washington 15 months ago. Secondly, we are reminded that al-Qaida and its associates are involved in a long-term struggle.

For al-Qaida, the Gulf remains the focus

In such a context, what is the significance of the attacks in Kenya? Two issues come to the fore immediately. The first is that the attacks largely failed but, if they had succeeded, would have been the most devastating incidents since 11 September 2001. The bombing of the hotel was intended to kill scores of Israeli tourists who had just arrived. Instead, the timing was wrong, the tourists had checked into the hotel and had dispersed to their rooms. As a result, most of those killed were young members of a Kenyan dance group.

The attempt to destroy the passenger jet using shoulder-launched missiles was intended to kill over 200 people, an atrocity that would have been by far the largest loss of life for the Israelis in a single incident in the 54-year history of the country. Causing this loss of life when a singularly hawkish administration was in power would almost inevitably have involved an extreme Israeli military response.

Successive Israeli governments have been particularly uncompromising when it comes to attacks on Israeli citizens abroad. Although the invasion of Lebanon in 1982 was already being planned, it was prompted as a response to the attempted assassination of the Israeli Ambassador to Britain.

As it is, considerable US pressure is being exerted on the Sharon government to refrain from such action, but this will not be easy. There is a widespread feeling of insecurity in Israel because of the many bombings, though still a certain perception of safety when people are travelling abroad on holiday. Going by Israeli-owned charter jets to Israeli-owned hotels was presumed safe. With hindsight, the very identity of these facilities actually made them clear-cut targets for a paramilitary movement with extensive international resources.

Even so, we have to go beyond these immediate attacks to get a clearer idea of the strategy of al-Qaida and its associates. Here is the second area where the Kenyan incidents offer wider significance.

At root, the al-Qaida network is involved in a long-term programme aimed at creating a wider and more coherent Islamic world based on a particularly rigorous interpretation of Islam that is not shared by the great majority of Muslims. Within this overall intention, two specific and more short-term objectives are the determination to expel American forces from the Gulf and the ending of the Saudi monarchy's control of Saudi Arabia.

Even this is quite a long-term programme, already underway for a decade and with another decade in prospect before it might be achieved, but it is part of a much longer strategy that might stretch over half a century, beyond the lifespans of the main participants. For the moment, though, the Gulf, US influence and the House of Saud remain the main targets of al-Qaida's focus.

Entangling the US – and Israel?

In this mind-set, Israel and Iraq have been relatively unimportant until recently. The Israeli-Palestinian confrontation may cause endemic ill-feeling across the region, but al-Qaida has not been a ready supporter of the Palestinian cause, and this may well be for regional social reasons. Ever since the start of the Palestinian refugee problems in 1948, very large numbers of Palestinians have sought recourse to education as a way out of their marginalisation. This has been the case right through to university level; one result has been a diaspora of highly educated Palestinians, many of whom have gone on to be the professionals running public services throughout the Gulf.

While their presence has been indispensable to the economic development of the region, their sheer competence has frequently been resented, especially as young nationals of the Gulf states have more recently found it difficult to establish themselves in the professions at a time of relative economic recession.

The accumulated result of these trends has been that al-Qaida's natural sources of support have not been particularly positive towards the Palestinians; yet even this has been overcome by the hard-line policies of the Sharon government, such that al-Qaida has now embraced Israel as one of its core enemies, a process made so much easier by the prevailing regional perception of Israel as nothing more than a client state of Washington, using American bombers and helicopters to kill Palestinians.

Similarly, there was no great affinity between al-Qaida and Iraq, with the Saddam Hussein regime seen as an unacceptably secular state at the heart of the Islamic world. Even this antagonism has now been overcome, with al-Qaida now speaking out in favour of Iraq almost entirely because Baghdad is now in the sights of the Washington security hawks.

Indeed, by taking this line, al-Qaida will seek to gain substantially from the destruction of the Iraqi regime by the United States. Even the immediate collapse of the regime at the onset of a war would result in its replacement with a client state, and this would be represented as further proof of al-Qaida's long-term claim that the United States is utterly intent on controlling the region, in concert with Israel. A more disastrous war, with heavy civilian casualties and US forces tied down for many weeks or even months, would be an absolute gift to the organisation.

This leads us on to a general feature of the strategy that still seems largely unrecognised. This is that al-Qaida is specifically interested in inciting greater US and western military action anywhere in the Islamic world. It is not expecting to 'defeat' the United States in the short term. Quite the contrary – it positively seeks an increased confrontation as a means of greatly increasing support for both its medium-term and longer-term aims.

The Mombasa attacks therefore serve two purposes. One is specifically to draw the Israelis further into a regional 'war on terror'. The other is to demonstrate, by attempting to shoot down an airliner, that the reach of al-Qaida and its associates is potentially world-wide.

Meanwhile, the view from Washington remains that this is an unconventional war that can be fought and won on American terms. There is still little interest in understanding where al-Qaida is coming from or why support for it may even be increasing. The tragedy is that it may take more atrocities and much more loss of life before that understanding begins to dawn.

Afterword

An assessment of US policy in the 'war on terror' is best done in the context of the security attitudes of the incoming Bush administration in 2001 and the domestic impact of the World Trade Center and Pentagon attacks nine months later. While the Bush administration had been expected to adopt a consensual style of politics, not least because of the very narrow margin of victory, the reality was the vigorous pursuit of an independent and strongly unilateral path. Multilateral agreements were of value only when they were in the direct interests of the United States, otherwise they were seen primarily as a hindrance in the pursuit of policy.

In terms of the international security agenda, a relatively narrow group of neo-conservatives had unusual influence, with this forming part of a wider belief that the United States had an historic mission to promote a 'New American Century' in which the world community would follow a path towards free market democracies, led and controlled by the United States. Even within eight months of taking office, such a view was being reflected across wide sectors of the administration, not least because of the evident position of the United States as the world's sole superpower.

The attacks in New York and Washington therefore came as profound shocks to a leadership community that had not begun to anticipate such vulnerability, and the immediate result was the need to adopt a vigorous policy designed to regain control. In a remarkable way, the 9/11 atrocities reinforced the neo-conservative paradigm rather than causing any kind of serious rethink, and an immediate consequence of this was the military operation to terminate the Taliban regime and the al-Qaida network within Afghanistan.

That process appeared initially successful and, by January 2002, the policy of regaining control had extended beyond the immediate 'war on terror' to address the issue of 'rogue' states, not least in terms of the threat from the proliferation of nuclear, chemical and biological weapons and ballistic missiles.

In addition to a range of robust military and security postures, including large-scale detentions and even policies of selected assassination, defence budgets were increased, new military bases were developed in regions of concern, and there was a particular concentration on the security of the Persian Gulf in general and the problem of Iraq in particular. In this context, Israel retained its importance for the United States, in spite of the hard-line policies being pursued by the Sharon government.

In the latter months of 2002, however, pursuit of many of the policies was already beginning to prove problematic. In Afghanistan, it became clear that many Taliban units had successfully dispersed, as had al-Qaida members, and the leadership of both groups remained largely at liberty. The country itself was in some disarray, and al-Qaida and its affiliates had either moved on or were already active in a number of other countries.

While the attacks in New York and Washington had resulted in initial sympathy for the United States, much of this evaporated within six months in the face of an administration in Washington that seemed intent on following its own policies regardless of the views of others, even if they were normally considered to be trusted allies. This suspicion even extended to a number of key European states, especially when the US maintained support for Israel during the latter's harsh military incursions into the occupied territories early in 2002.

By the latter part of 2002, attention had, in any case, moved on to Iraq, with clear indications that the Bush administration was intent on regime termination. This aroused opposition across the world, both directly, in terms of what was planned, and indirectly in that many governments believed it to be a dangerous diversion that might prove counterproductive to regional and international security.

Whatever the validity of such a view, it was unacceptable in Washington and regime termination went ahead, on the stated basis of being necessary to destroy Iraq's arsenal of weapons of mass destruction. The initial Iraq War and consequent destruction of the regime took barely three weeks, but killed some 6,000 civilians and an even higher number of Iraqi soldiers. Contrary to pre-war expectations, the US forces and their British assistants were scarcely welcomed as liberators, and immediate post-war problems of chaotic services and a severely damaged economy added to a predicament in which liberation was replaced by perceived occupation. This was made worse by serious and violent resistance coming from Ba'athist and other elements, leading to hundreds of deaths and injuries for US troops.

As the second anniversary of the 9/11 attacks approaches, problems persist in Iraq and in relation to al-Qaida. Opposition to what is widely seen in the Arab world as the foreign occupation of a major Arab state is so far coming primarily from internal Iraqi elements, but it is a reasonable prediction that it will serve to enhance wider regional support for of al-Qaida and affiliated paramilitary organisations. Indeed, the location of well over 100,000 American soldiers as an occupying force in the heart of the Middle East is essentially likely to provide paramilitaries with ready targets for a long time to come.

In Afghanistan, post-war reconstruction has proved deeply problematic as the ISAF soldiers remain restricted to the area around Kabul, US troops continue to meet guerrilla opposition, and much of the country is in the hands of warlords with no allegiance to the nominal government of the country. Taliban elements remain very much at large and a substantial US military presence seems set to continue for some years to come. Furthermore, al-Qaida and its associated groups remain active, with substantial attacks in Casablanca, Riyadh and Djakarta all demonstrating a capability that cannot be said to be under control.

Looking at President Bush's 'war on terror' some two years after the 9/11 attacks, it is reasonable to say that the United States is less popular and substantially less respected across the world, has failed to ensure post-war stability in Afghanistan, faces further problems from paramilitary organisations and has found it unexpectedly difficult to maintain control in Iraq. Moreover, its own concentration on homeland security, coupled with regular warnings of possible attacks, suggests that even the security of its own country is far from assured.

Even so, there is little in the way of any indication that the Bush administration is able to comprehend the predicament in which it finds itself, still less is it able to address the root causes of paramilitarism and the reasons why groups such as al-Qaida maintain their support. In such circumstances, it would be wise to assume that, until there are profound changes in outlook and understanding, the United States is unlikely to experience greater security. Given its vigorous and global approach to maintaining control, this is a circumstance that has implications for the whole global community.

Index